One world under surveillance

By Mathew Henderson

About the author

Mathew Henderson is a Technology Strategy Consultant, recognized for his expertise in crafting effective digital and data strategies for prominent large corporates and government agencies worldwide. Based in New Zealand, he has honed his skills over years of experience, delivering valuable insights and innovative solutions that have had a significant impact on the organizations he serves.

Specializing in the ever-evolving landscape of digital and data management, Mathew has collaborated with diverse clients across various industries, leveraging cutting-edge technologies to drive business growth and optimize operational efficiencies. His strategic guidance and practical implementation have led to measurable successes for his clients, enhancing their competitiveness and positioning them at the forefront of their respective sectors.

Through his work with global corporations and government agencies, Mathew has gained an exceptional understanding of the intricate dynamics between data, technology, and governance. His firsthand involvement in shaping digital transformation initiatives has provided him with unique perspectives on the challenges and opportunities posed by modern surveillance practices.

In light of his involvement in the digital realm, Mathew's views on surveillance have developed over the years. He recognizes the importance of balancing data-driven insights and privacy concerns in today's interconnected world. His experiences have led him to advocate for ethical and responsible data governance, emphasizing the critical significance of safeguarding individual liberties while harnessing the potential of data-driven decision-making and ensuring that organizations harness the power of data while respecting individual rights and freedoms.

One world under surveillance

Introduction

"The measure of a man is what he does with power."

Plato

It is a true-ism to say we are experiencing profound technological advancements and interconnectedness, however we are and the world finds itself at the crossroads of significant change. The magnitude of which is unprecedented in our history as a species.

Although the drivers and results of that ongoing change are not always clear, one aspect has emerged with rapid ferocity and is now quite resolvable to those who wish to look. It is of course the trend of State and Commercial surveillance.

The landscape of surveillance has become ubiquitous, reshaping the very foundations of our social fabric. This book serves as a guide, shedding light on the complexities of surveillance, online monitoring, and the real and potential impact on individuals and communities. Through a meticulous exploration of definitions, prevalence, and consequences, I have aimed to provide some sense of navigate the uncharted territories of this evolving paradigm for the benefit of others and not least for my own benefit in thinking through this issue.

Surveillance, in its broadest sense, encompasses the systematic observation, monitoring, and gathering of information about individuals or groups. Online monitoring, specifically tailored to the digital realm, encompasses practices such as data collection, tracking, and profiling individuals' online activities. Understanding these definitions lays the groundwork for comprehending the far-reaching extent of surveillance in our contemporary society.

Privacy and security, long-standing cornerstones of societal order, and assume an even greater significance in our rapidly changing world. Privacy has always provided individuals with the freedom to express themselves, foster intimate relationships, and maintain personal autonomy. Conversely, security serves as the guardian against external threats, fostering trust and stability within communities. Balancing these values is pivotal for a harmonious and equitable society, one that cherishes both individual rights and collective well-being.

This book is a humble attempt to delve into the intricate relationship between surveillance, privacy, and security. Though not an expert in the field, my professional endeavours in corporate strategic planning with a focus on digital technologies have often skirted these topics. As my understanding deepened, I felt compelled to pen my thoughts, both as a means of personal reflection and as a warning to others. The immense shift we are witnessing in society propelled me to explore what insights I could make out, and hopefully in the process urging readers to contemplate the consequences of this transformation.

The basis of political power and the rationale for the states existence have evolved over time. Once rooted in traditional realms such as military capability and provision of security is undergoing a foundational change. Although this rationale for its existence remains, the foundations are increasingly becoming information-based. In a post 911 online world, granular insights as to individual motives and actions have become equally important to governments and commercial interests alike. The revelations of Edward Snowden in his book *permanent record* demonstrated the extent and depth of these profiles on individuals that governments and corporates create and monitor. Without checks and balances the looming potential for an Orwellian world beckons on the horizon. However as responsible and informed citizens, we have the capacity to harness this paradigm shift for the greater good while safeguarding against its potential negative consequences. Through knowledge, critical thinking, and engagement, we can shape the future and navigate the intricate intersection of surveillance, privacy, and security.

In the chapters that follow, I aim to provide and backdrop of the current issues of concern, as well as the positive developments, many of which are not self evident or visible in our daily lives. In doing so we delve into the historical context of surveillance, ponder its ethical implications, examine the legal frameworks that attempt to regulate it, and unravel its profound impact on individuals and communities. We also confront the technological advances that propel surveillance forward and explore the delicate dance between surveillance and digital freedom. Lastly, we will focus on perhaps the most important aspect of the book, what we as individuals and collectively as groups do about these developments. .

Unfortunately, these technologies, international agreements, and uses do put our cherished freedoms at risk. In order to shape the future we want of our societies we need to inform ourselves and stay vigilant, for the choices we make in this will shape the world we inhabit. Through understanding, introspection, and responsible action, we can strive to strike a delicate equilibrium between privacy, security, and the currently rapidly encroaching realm of surveillance.

Mathew Henderson, Auckland New Zealand
July 2023

Chapter 1
Chapter One the rise of CCTV

"Big Brother is watching you."

George Orwell, 1984

Closed Circuit Television (CCTV) technology has come a long way since it was first developed in the 1940s. Originally used for military purposes, CCTV has become increasingly ubiquitous in public places, workplaces, and homes. This chapter will examine how CCTV technology has evolved over time and how it has become so prevalent in our society today.

Early developments

The earliest versions of CCTV technology were developed during World War II for military purposes, including the use of Closed-circuit television (CCTV) to monitor the launch of V-2 rockets from Germany to the United Kingdom. The use of CCTV in military applications began in the 1940s, with the aim of improving surveillance and intelligence-gathering capabilities.
The technology was first used to monitor the launch of V-2 rockets, which were the world's first long-range guided ballistic missiles, capable of traveling at a speed of up to 5,760 km/h (3,580 mph). The rockets were launched from various locations in Germany and were targeted at cities in the UK. In response, the British government established a number of observation posts and radar stations to detect and track the incoming missiles. CCTV was used as part of this system to provide real-time surveillance of the launches and to help identify the launching sites.
One of the most famous applications of CCTV during World War II was the use of the technology to monitor the D-Day landings in 1944. In the lead-up to the landings, the Allies used CCTV to observe German troop movements and to identify potential landing sites. The technology was also used to monitor the progress of the landings themselves, providing real-time intelligence to commanders in the field.

These early CCTV systems were simple by today's standards, consisting of a single camera connected to a monitor. However, the technology continued to evolve throughout the 20th century. In the 1970s, VCR technology was integrated into CCTV systems, allowing footage to be recorded for later viewing. This was a significant development as it enabled CCTV footage to be used as evidence in criminal investigations.

Over time, the use of CCTV technology expanded beyond military and government applications. In 1949, the first commercial use of CCTV was in a department store in the UK to monitor shoplifters. This was followed by the installation of CCTV systems in banks, casinos, and other high-security facilities. In the 1970s and 1980s, CCTV became more widely used in public places, such as train stations and city centers, as a way of deterring crime and improving public safety[1]

Analog CCTV

Analog CCTV technology, which transmitted video signals from a camera to a monitor, was developed in the 1960s. At that time, the technology was expensive and required skilled technicians to install and maintain it. However, by the 1970s, analog CCTV systems became more affordable and were widely adopted for security and surveillance purposes.
Initially, analog CCTV systems were used primarily in banks and government buildings. These early systems consisted of a camera, a coaxial cable to transmit the video signal, and a monitor to display the image. The technology was complex and required skilled technicians to install and maintain it, making it expensive and limiting its use.

One of the earliest uses of analog CCTV was by the New York City Police Department in the 1960s. They installed cameras in high-crime areas, hoping to deter crime by creating a visual presence. However, the results were mixed, and the system was criticized for being too expensive and for invading people's privacy.

Another early use of analog CCTV was in the United Kingdom. The first CCTV system in the UK was installed in 1965 in the town of Bournemouth. The system consisted of ten cameras placed around the town, transmitting their signals back to a central control room. The system was installed to combat vandalism and theft, and it was deemed a success.
In the 1970s, analog CCTV systems became more affordable and widely adopted. The technology had improved, and it was now easier to install and maintain. As a result, businesses began to adopt the technology for security and surveillance purposes.

One example of this was the use of analog CCTV by retail stores to prevent shoplifting. The cameras were installed in prominent locations and monitored by security personnel. The cameras acted as a deterrent to would-be thieves, and the footage could be used as evidence in court.

Another example of the widespread adoption of analog CCTV was in public transportation systems. Buses and trains were equipped with cameras to monitor passenger behavior, prevent vandalism, and ensure the safety of passengers.

---

[1] "Closed-Circuit Television (CCTV) in the UK." History of Surveillance in the UK, www.surveillance-studies.org/closed-circuit-television-cctv-uk/., "CCTV." Imperial War Museums, www.iwm.org.uk/history/cctv., "Surveillance and Security: Technological and Social Dimensions." Annual Review of Sociology, vol. 35, 2009, pp. 193–217.

The development of analog CCTV technology also led to the creation of closed-circuit television networks (CCTV). These networks allowed multiple cameras to be connected to a single control room, where security personnel could monitor the footage from each camera. This allowed for more comprehensive surveillance of large areas, such as airports or industrial facilities. While analog CCTV technology had become more affordable and easier to install, it still had limitations. The cameras had a fixed field of view and were unable to zoom in or out. The images captured by the cameras were also of lower quality compared to modern digital cameras.

Analog CCTV technology was developed in the 1960s and was initially expensive and required skilled technicians to install and maintain it. However, by the 1970s, the technology had improved, and it became more affordable and widely adopted for security and surveillance purposes. Analog CCTV systems were used in a variety of settings, from banks and government buildings to retail stores and public transportation systems. The technology paved the way for the development of closed-circuit television networks, allowing for more comprehensive surveillance of large areas. Despite its limitations, analog CCTV technology was a significant step forward in the evolution of surveillance technology[2].

Digital CCTV

The development of digital CCTV systems has revolutionized the way we use video surveillance. Digital CCTV systems use digital technology to convert analog signals into digital data, which can be stored on a computer hard drive. This has several advantages over traditional analog CCTV systems, including higher-quality images, remote access, and more sophisticated analytics. Digital CCTV systems are more reliable than analog systems because they are less susceptible to interference and signal degradation. This means that digital images are clearer and more consistent, even when recorded over long periods of time. The use of digital technology also allows for more flexibility in terms of camera placement and system configuration.
One example of the advantages of digital CCTV systems is the ability to remotely access live or recorded footage from anywhere with an internet connection. This allows for real-time monitoring and quick response times to security incidents. Additionally, digital CCTV systems

[2] References:

"The History and Evolution of CCTV Technology" by Essential Systems Inc.
"A Brief History of CCTV" by SPT Security Systems
"The Development of CCTV" by InTouch CCTV Systems

can be integrated with other security technologies such as access control and alarm systems, allowing for a more comprehensive security solution.

Digital CCTV systems also allow for more sophisticated analytics than analog systems. For example, facial recognition technology can be used to identify individuals and track their movements within a camera's field of view. This technology has been used to catch criminals and prevent terrorist attacks, but it also raises concerns about privacy and civil liberties.

In addition to facial recognition, digital CCTV systems can also use other types of analytics such as license plate recognition and object tracking. License plate recognition technology can be used to identify vehicles and track their movements, which is useful for law enforcement and parking enforcement. Object tracking can be used to detect and track specific objects such as bags or packages, which can help prevent theft or other security incidents.

The development of digital CCTV systems has also led to the growth of the video surveillance market. According to a report by ResearchAndMarkets.com, the global video surveillance market was valued at $58.45 billion in 2020 and is expected to reach $99.28 billion by 2026. This growth is driven by the increasing need for security in various industries such as retail, banking, and transportation.

However, the use of digital CCTV systems has also raised concerns about privacy and civil liberties. The ability to remotely access footage and use sophisticated analytics raises questions about who has access to this data and how it is being used. There have been several high-profile cases of data breaches involving video surveillance footage, which highlights the need for strong data protection measures.

The development of digital CCTV systems has transformed the way we use video surveillance for security and surveillance purposes. The advantages of digital technology include higher-quality images, remote access, and more sophisticated analytics. However, this technology also raises concerns about privacy and civil liberties. It is important to balance the benefits of digital CCTV systems with the need for strong data protection measures to ensure that this technology is used in a responsible and ethical manner[3].

IP-based CCTV

---

[3] "Video Surveillance Market - Growth, Trends, COVID-19 Impact, and Forecasts (2021 - 2026)" by ResearchAndMarkets.com, "The Advantages of Digital Video Surveillance" by Security Today, "The Pros and Cons of Digital CCTV Systems" by IFSEC Global

The latest development in CCTV technology is IP-based CCTV. IP-based CCTV systems use the internet protocol to transmit video signals over a network. This technology allows for remote access, higher-quality images, and easier integration with other digital systems. IP-based CCTV has become the preferred choice for many businesses and organizations due to its flexibility and scalability.

Ubiquitous presence

CCTV technology has become ubiquitous in public places, workplaces, and homes. It is estimated that there are approximately 350 million CCTV cameras in use worldwide. In the UK alone, there are over 5 million CCTV cameras, which is equivalent to one camera for every 13 people.

Public Places

It is common for CCTV technology to be used in public places such as airports, train stations, shopping malls, and public streets in order to provide security to the general public.CCTV cameras are used for monitoring crowds, preventing crime, collecting evidence, and deterring criminal behavior. Often, they are installed in high-risk areas, such as parking lots and public transportation hubs, in order to improve the safety of the general public.

There is no doubt that CCTV technology has become an integral part of ensuring workplace security and surveillance in recent years.There has been a growing use of CCTV cameras in workplaces over the past few years due to a rise in employee theft and the need to maintain a secure environment in the workplace as a result of increasing employee theft.With the help of this technology, the company is able to monitor employee behavior, prevent theft, and ensure compliance with the company's policies.Cameras are often installed in areas where sensitive or confidential information is stored, such as server rooms and research labs, to ensure that these areas are secure and can only be accessed by authorized personnel in order to ensure that the information is protected.

A typical example of how CCTV cameras are used in the workplace is in the banking industry.The banks are required to maintain a secure environment in order to ensure the safety of their customers' funds and personal information on a day-to-day basis.It is common practice for banks to install CCTV cameras in order to monitor employee behavior and prevent fraudulent activities, such as theft and money laundering.Furthermore, banks also use CCTV cameras to monitor their ATMs in order to prevent vandalism or theft from occurring.

Manufacturing plants are another example of a workplace where CCTV technology is being used to keep an eye on the workers.It is not uncommon for CCTV cameras to be installed in various areas of a manufacturing plant in order to monitor employee behavior, prevent theft, and ensure compliance with safety regulations and guidelines.An example of this would be in a factory where heavy machinery is used, CCTV cameras are installed to ensure the safety of the employees and ensure that they comply with safety protocols in order to ensure their safety. In addition to CCTV cameras being used in schools and universities, they are also used to ensure the safety of students and staff at these institutions.The recent spate of school shootings has led to the installation of CCTV cameras around the premises of many educational institutions as a result of several incidents.In order to ensure that no unauthorized individuals are present on campus, these cameras monitor entrances and exits, hallways, and other common areas to ensure that no unauthorized individuals are present.

The retail industry is another example of a place where CCTV cameras are used to monitor a variety of activities.It is common for retail stores to use CCTV cameras in order to monitor their employees and prevent theft from happening.In retail stores, CCTV cameras are installed in order to monitor the behavior of the employees and to make sure they are providing good customer service to the customers.In addition to this, CCTV cameras are also used to monitor the customers and prevent theft from taking place.There is a tendency for retailers to install CCTV cameras at the entrances and exits of their stores in order to monitor their customers as they enter and exit the store.

Without a doubt, CCTV technology has become one of the most indispensable tools when it comes to securing, monitoring, and ensuring the security of the workplace and ensuring its safety. At some point, however, it becomes necessary to ask whether the level of usage and ubiquity of this technology has not reached a tipping point that may result in more harm than good in the long run.In the majority of the industries and settings today, CCTV cameras are widely used in order to monitor employees and prevent theft, as well as to ensure compliance with safety regulations and regulations in order to ensure employee safety, which has become a common practice over the past few years. However, the flip side to this is that as technology continues to develop, more and more data is being collected from these devices as a result, and given the digital nature of these data sets, these data sets can easily be packaged, integrated, and sold or provided to third parties for marketing or for government surveillance purposes.It is important to note that in order to make use of any technology and its application in a balanced manner, both in terms of the way the technology is used and how it is applied.It is, therefore, important that we ask ourselves as a society whether we have crossed that balance, and if so, are we now past the point of no return? In light of this, one of the questions we need to answer is: Have we crossed that balance yet?

Homes

One of the more recent developments is that CCTV technology is increasingly being used in homes as a part of their security systems.The main purpose of CCTV cameras is to monitor the property of the homeowner as well as to deter crime from happening.In addition to being able to be installed both indoors and outdoors, they can be connected to a home network for remote access as well.There is no doubt that CCTV cameras have become an indispensable part of many home security systems, providing homeowners with a sense of security and peace of mind.There are, however, the same problems with balance that exist for these installations as well.The majority of these devices are sold as wirelessly enabled items that can be easily installed on a phone and there are no wires to be tangled.However, due to the fact that these devices are Wi-Fi enabled, and as a result, they can be a significant security risk to home networks as a result.Considering the fact that wi-fi enabled devices can be hacked from outside of the home, it is technically possible to spy on the goings and comings of the occupants from the outside of the home without them knowing that anything is happening.Once again, it is important to make a trade-off between the benefits and the risks involved, and it is a very personal choice that needs to be made based on your own preferences.In addition to that, it is also a choice that should be made in the context of understanding the risks that might be involved in that decision.

CCTV technology has come a long way since its development in the 1940s. From its early use in military and commercial applications to the emergence of digital and IP-based systems, CCTV technology has become an essential tool for security and surveillance in public places, workplaces, and homes. While there are concerns about the impact of ubiquitous CCTV on privacy, it is clear that CCTV technology has become an integral part of our modern society. As technology continues to evolve, it is likely that CCTV technology will continue to play a significant role in public safety and security.

Chapter 2
The ethics of surveillance

"The greatest danger to liberty lurks in insidious encroachment by men of zeal, well-meaning but without understanding."

Louis Brandeis - U.S. Supreme Court Justice

Surveillance abuse: governments and corporations in the modern age

The modern world is governed by surveillance, with governments and corporations utilizing sophisticated technologies to monitor individuals and collect vast amounts of personal information. Public safety and efficiency are often the goals of surveillance, but its abuse is a growing concern. This chapter explores real-life examples of how governments and corporations have abused surveillance, infringed on privacy rights and wielding excessive power over individuals.

Governments worldwide have increasingly engaged in controversial surveillance practices that raise ethical and legal concerns[4]. Edward Snowden's 2013 revelations about surveillance programs are one notable example. National Security Agency (NSA) surveillance in the United States, which involved the mass collection of phone records and internet communications of Americans and foreigners, was exposed by Snowden. The revelations prompted global debate on the balance between national security and privacy rights, revealing how governments can violate individual liberties in the name of security. Additionally, Snowden released documents related to the five eyes alliance's day-to-day operations.

The Five Eyes Alliance is an international intelligence-sharing partnership comprising five English-speaking countries: the United States, the United Kingdom, Canada, Australia, and New Zealand. Established during the post-World War II era, the alliance aimed to enhance intelligence cooperation among these countries. However, the Five Eyes alliance has evolved over the years into a robust and comprehensive global surveillance network. Its extent and

---

[4] https://www.ohchr.org/en/press-releases/2022/09/spyware-and-surveillance-threats-privacy-and-human-rights-growing-un-report

reach are now so large that real and valid concerns about privacy, civil liberties, and its capabilities are forefront in the minds of many leaders.

The agreement dates back to 1946 when the United Kingdom and the United States signed the UK-USA Agreement[5]. Following the passage of the 1943 Britain–United States of America agreement (BRUSA)[6], the United Kingdom and the United States officially enacted the secret treaty on 5 March 1946 following an informal agreement related to the 1941 Atlantic Charter. A major focus of the agreement was on signals intelligence (SIGINT) and code-breaking. In the following years, it was extended to encompass Canada, Australia, and New Zealand, and the partnership was formalized and deepened. Other countries, known as "third parties", such as West Germany, the Philippines, and several Nordic countries, also joined the UKUSA community in associate capacities. However, they are not part of the mechanism between the Five Eyes related to automatically sharing of data and insights.

During the Cold War, the Five Eyes alliance played an important role in monitoring and countering Soviet activities. As part of the alliance's surveillance efforts, communications were intercepted and analyzed, intelligence was collected, and information was exchanged. It became a vital asset in collecting signals intelligence, including telephone conversations, emails, and other forms of electronic communication.

Today, the alliance possesses surveillance capabilities that allow it to conduct intelligence activities on a global scale. This includes monitoring foreign and domestic communications, collecting vast amounts of data, and analyzing it for intelligence. The alliance relies on advanced technology, such as sophisticated data interception systems, satellite communications, and robust data processing and analysis tools. The current capabilities of the Five Eyes Alliance extend well beyond the original scope of SIGINT. With the rise of digital communications and the proliferation of internet-based technologies, the alliance has adapted its surveillance techniques to encompass a wide range of online activities. This includes the interception and analysis of internet traffic, monitoring of social media platforms, and the collection of metadata, which can provide valuable insights into individuals' communication patterns and connections.

Over time, the five eyes partner nations created a global surveillance network code-named "ECHELON" in 1971.In the aftermath of the 1970s Watergate affair and a subsequent congressional inquiry led by Sen. Frank Church,[8] it was revealed that the NSA, in collaboration with Britain's GCHQ, had routinely intercepted the international communications of prominent anti-Vietnam War leaders such as Jane Fonda and Dr. Benjamin Spock.[9] Decades later, a multi-year investigation by the European Parliament highlighted the NSA's role in economic espionage in a report entitled 'Development of Surveillance Technology and Risk of Abuse of Economic Information', in 1999.[10].

---

5 https://en.wikipedia.org/wiki/UKUSA_Agreement

6 https://en.wikipedia.org/wiki/1943_BRUSA_Agreement#cite_note-1

In the 1970s, the five eye partner nations developed a global surveillance system code-named ECHELON. After the Watergate affair and a subsequent congressional inquiry led by Sen. Frank Church,[8] revealed that the NSA had routinely intercepted the international communications of prominent anti-Vietnam War leaders like Jane Fonda and Dr. Benjamin Spock, working with Britain's GCHQ. An investigation by the European Parliament in 1999 titled 'Development of Surveillance Technology and Risk of Abuse of Economic Information' highlighted the NSA's role in economic espionage decades later.

In June 2013, NSA documents detailing its foreign and domestic spying were made available to the public for the first time. The majority of these documents were leaked by Edward Snowden, an ex-contractor. Many of these older global surveillance programs, such as PRISM, XKeyscore, and Tempora, were referenced in the 2013 release of thousands of documents. The "Five Eyes" alliance of Australia, Canada, New Zealand, the UK, and the United States has targeted countries around the world, including Western Allies and NATO members. Using analytical tools such as the Boundless Informant, five English-speaking Western countries aim to achieve Total Information Awareness by mastering the Internet. On 26 September 2013, NSA director Keith B. Alexander confirmed that all phone records of all Americans are collected and stored. The Utah Data Center, a US $1.5 billion megaproject referred to as a "symbol of the spy agency's surveillance prowess," stores most of the data.

On 6 June 2013, Britain's The Guardian newspaper published a series of revelations by an as-yet-unknown American whistleblower. The whistleblower was revealed several days later to be ex-CIA and ex-NSA contractor Edward Snowden.Two journalists, Glenn Greenwald and Laura Poitras, received a cache of documents from Snowden. According to Greenwald, the cache contains 15,000–20,000 documents, some very detailed and large, some very small. A series of subsequent publications revealed that the NSA had operated a complex web of spying programs that allowed it to intercept Internet and telephone conversations from over a billion users in dozens of countries. The publication of documents reveals, however, that many of the programs indiscriminately collected bulk information directly from central servers and Internet backbones, which almost invariably carry and reroute data from distant countries.

ECHELON is believed to employ a vast network of interception stations and sophisticated analysis tools to sift through immense amounts of data, focusing on identifying keywords and patterns of interest. William Blum in his book Rogue State in 2005 wrote , "the ECHELON system works by indiscriminately intercepting huge quantities of communications and using computers to identify and extract messages of interest from the unwanted ones. Every intercepted message—all the embassy cables, the business deals, the sex talk, the birthday greetings—is searched for key words, which could be anything the searchers think might be of interest

The Five Eyes alliance also benefits from its expansive network of intelligence agencies and cooperative agreements with other countries. This allows for information sharing and collaborative surveillance efforts on a global scale.

Implications and concerns

Although the Five Eyes alliance might sound like the plot of a James Bond novel, its implications for the public are far from fiction. It is important to understand that this intelligence network is a two-edged sword for society as a whole and at an individual level. There is no doubt that it contributes to public safety by upholding national security and tackling global threats. Its price, however, is our privacy.

We live in a connected, digital world where surveillance for safety has blurred the line between privacy invasion and surveillance for safety. Snowden's 2013 revelations shed light on the alliance's extensive data harvesting activities, highlighting the precarious balance between security and individual privacy.

The digital footprints we leave behind, such as emails, phone calls, online shopping and social media activity, could potentially be open books, read without our knowledge or consent. Surveillance and civil liberties are closely intertwined in this stark reality, which fuels ongoing debates about privacy, state power, and the fine line between these issues.

Often, this argument is used to justify surveillance practices, suggesting those leading law-abiding lives shouldn't be concerned about privacy invasions.

However, this viewpoint is simplistic and overlooks a key aspect of privacy-it isn't just about hiding wrongdoing. In addition to controlling personal information, maintaining space where we can stay free of outside observation, and expressing opinions without fear of reprisal, privacy also involves the right to control personal information.

The extensive surveillance capabilities of the Five Eyes alliance raise significant concerns regarding privacy, civil liberties, and the potential for abuse. The alliance's ability to collect and analyze vast amounts of personal data, both domestically and internationally, raises questions about the scope of its operations and the extent to which privacy rights are being respected. The mass surveillance activities of the alliance have been criticized for infringing upon individual freedoms and eroding privacy expectations.

Moreover, the lack of transparency and oversight surrounding the Five Eyes Alliance's activities is a cause for concern. The secretive nature of the alliance makes it difficult to hold its member countries accountable for any potential abuses or violations of civil liberties. This raises questions about the balance between security and privacy and the need for robust legal frameworks and independent oversight to ensure that surveillance activities are conducted within ethical boundaries.

There is no doubt that the Five Eyes alliance plays a crucial role when it comes to global security, but it is equally important to remember that privacy is fundamental to democratic societies. Thus, the alliance's activities highlight the need for a delicate balance between security and individual rights-a balance that remains a major topic of discussion.

China's approach to surveillance is an interesting case study in how these capabilities can be deployed. A focal point of scrutiny is Xinjiang, China's largest province by territory and home to a significant Uighur Muslim population. Chinese government deployments of extensive surveillance infrastructure in Xinjiang are emblematic of a broader trend in leveraging technology for social control. This apparatus encompasses a multifaceted array of tools, ranging from ubiquitous facial recognition systems to the pervasive network of cameras strategically positioned across urban landscapes. Furthermore, sophisticated algorithms have been developed to sift through vast troves of data, enabling the authorities to monitor individuals' activities and movements, particularly Uighurs[7].

As evidenced by the litany of documented human rights violations, the ramifications of this surveillance regime go far beyond mere monitoring. According to reports, more than a million Uighur Muslims have been detained arbitrarily in "re-education camps"[8]. These facilities, shrouded in secrecy and devoid of due process, serve as instruments of cultural repression, aimed at erasing ethnic and religious identities that do not conform to the state's vision of homogeneity. Satellite imagery and testimonies from survivors have revealed the systemic abuse and indoctrination that took place within these facilities, painting a harrowing picture of state-sponsored oppression.

Xinjiang's surveillance apparatus is not an isolated phenomenon, but rather a part of China's broader strategy of social control. Beyond its borders, the Chinese government's surveillance capabilities extend to encompass virtually every facet of public and private life, facilitating the monitoring and censorship of online discourse and dissenting voices. This pervasive surveillance state serves as a potent tool in quelling any semblance of opposition, instilling a climate of fear and self-censorship among citizens wary of attracting the state's gaze.

Rather than being a matter of security or public safety, China's surveillance technology has morphed into a tool of authoritarian control. As a result of harnessing the power of advanced technology, the Chinese government has constructed an Orwellian dystopia in which individual freedoms are sacrificed to achieve state control. Despite the expansion of surveillance, it is

---

[7] https://www.sciencedirect.com/science/article/pii/S0160791X22002780

[8] https://www.independent.co.uk/news/world/asia/xi-jinping-regime-han-chinese-threat-uighur-muslims-persecution-detention-camps-a9051126.html

imperative to confront the ethical implications of these practices and protect the basic rights and dignity of everyone, regardless of ethnicity or creed.

Corporate surveillance

In the corporate world, surveillance abuse is predominantly driven by collecting and exploiting personal data for profit. Technology companies like Facebook and Google have been embroiled in numerous controversies regarding their data practices. In the Cambridge Analytica scandal, Facebook was found to have allowed unauthorized access to personal data from millions of its users. This data was exploited for targeted political advertising, undermining the democratic process. The incident exposed how corporations can manipulate and abuse personal data for financial gain, jeopardizing individuals' privacy and autonomy.

A concerning aspect of corporate surveillance[9] is the rise of surveillance capitalism[10], where companies profit by capturing, analyzing, and selling individuals' personal information. This practice extends beyond social media platforms to encompass various industries, including retail, insurance, and healthcare. The increasing integration of surveillance technologies, such as smart devices and IoT (Internet of Things) systems, enables companies to gather detailed information about individuals' behaviors, preferences, and physical health. This exploitation of personal data erodes privacy rights and creates a pervasive surveillance culture. Surveillance abuse becomes particularly alarming when governments and corporations collaborate to further their mutual interests. The Snowden leaks revealed the extent of cooperation between intelligence agencies and technology companies, highlighting the intricate relationship between state surveillance and corporate data collection. These partnerships raise concerns about the erosion of privacy rights and the potential for abuse of power when governments and corporations combine their surveillance capabilities. One notable example is the collaboration between intelligence agencies and telecommunications companies in various countries. The revelations surrounding the PRISM program demonstrated how technology companies granted the government direct access to their users' data, bypassing legal

---

[9] Price, D. H. (2014). The New Surveillance Normal: NSA and Corporate Surveillance in the Age of Global Capitalism. *Monthly Review, 66*(3), 43. https://doi.org/10.14452/mr-066-03-2014-07_3

[10] Zuboff, S. (2019). *The Age of Surveillance Capitalism: The fight for a human future at the new frontier of power.* https://cds.cern.ch/record/2655106

safeguards. This collusion undermines individuals' trust in both governments and corporations, as their private communications and personal information are compromised without their knowledge or consent.

Democracy and surveillance

Any democratic society should adhere to the principle of transparency[11]. By making citizens aware of the extent and purpose of surveillance practices, they can make informed privacy decisions. Despite this, governments and corporations have often collected vast amounts of personal data without explicit consent due to the pervasive nature of surveillance. This raises the potential for abuse of power and the violation of individual rights.

The concept of accountability is another crucial factor that needs to be taken into account when dealing with surveillance[12]. Robust mechanisms must be in place to ensure that governments or law enforcement agencies do not abuse surveillance powers. The absence of effective oversight and accountability can lead to the erosion of civil liberties and the creation of a surveillance state. Therefore, it is imperative to balance security concerns and protecting individual rights. Consent is a cornerstone of ethical surveillance practices, and individuals should have the right to determine how their personal information is collected, stored, and used. However, obtaining informed consent has become increasingly challenging. Many online services and applications rely on complex terms and conditions, often burying consent clauses deep within lengthy documents. This raises questions about whether true consent is being obtained or if individuals are coerced into accepting pervasive surveillance practices.

The role of surveillance in the fight against crime and terrorism

Surveillance proponents argue it is vital in maintaining public safety and combating crime and terrorism. Surveillance technologies, such as CCTV cameras, facial recognition systems, and data analysis algorithms, are believed to enhance the capabilities of law enforcement agencies.

---

[11] Rothstein, B., & Teorell, J. (2008). What is quality of government? A theory of impartial government institutions. *Governance, 21*(2), 165–190. https://doi.org/10.1111/j.1468-0491.2008.00391.x

[12] Soldatov, A., & Borogan, I. (2013). Russia's surveillance state. *World Policy Journal, 30*(3), 23–30. https://doi.org/10.1177/0740277513506378

These tools can help detect and prevent criminal activities, leading to the swift apprehension of offenders and a safer society.

Law enforcement agencies assert that surveillance technologies are necessary to combat modern-day threats like terrorism and organized crime effectively. They argue that the ability to monitor public spaces and analyze vast amounts of data can provide valuable intelligence, helping them identify potential risks and take preemptive action. Moreover, proponents highlight numerous success stories where surveillance has aided in arresting and prosecuting dangerous criminals.

However, critics raise concerns about the potential for abuse and the erosion of civil liberties. They argue that the widespread use of surveillance technologies can create a surveillance state[13] where the government has unprecedented access to citizens' private lives. This concentration of power raises fears about the infringement of individual freedoms and the erosion of democratic values.

The debate over the necessity and effectiveness of surveillance

The necessity and effectiveness of surveillance technologies are subjects of intense debate. Proponents argue that surveillance is essential in maintaining public safety, deterring criminal activities, and enhancing national security. They point to instances where surveillance has proven effective in preventing and solving crimes, providing strong justification for its continued use.

On the other hand, critics contend that the benefits of surveillance are often overstated while the potential harms are downplayed. They argue that collecting vast amounts of personal data raises serious privacy concerns and creates the risk of abuse by both state and non-state actors. Moreover, critics question the effectiveness of surveillance in preventing crime and terrorism, pointing out that most surveillance systems are primarily reactive rather than proactive. The rapid advancement of surveillance technologies, such as facial recognition and predictive analytics[14], has intensified the debate. These emerging tools can potentially revolutionize surveillance practices and raise significant ethical issues.

---

[13] Greenwald, G. (2014). *No place to Hide: Edward Snowden, the NSA, and the U.S. Surveillance State*. http://ci.nii.ac.jp/ncid/BB18766657

[14] Chochia, A., & Nässi, T. (2021). Ethics and emerging technologies – facial recognition. *IDP*, *34*, 1–12. https://doi.org/10.7238/idp.v0i34.387466

Facial recognition technology, for instance, has sparked controversies due to concerns over accuracy, bias, and potential misuse. Studies have shown that these systems can be prone to errors, particularly when identifying individuals from minority groups. This raises serious concerns about the potential for discriminatory targeting and false accusations based on flawed surveillance data.

Furthermore, using predictive analytics in surveillance has raised ethical questions about the presumption of innocence and the potential for profiling[15]. Predictive algorithms analyze vast amounts of data to identify patterns and predict future behavior. While this can be useful in identifying potential threats, it also risks labelling innocent individuals as suspects based on algorithmic predictions, undermining the principle of due process.

A strong argument against the widespread use of surveillance is its very real impact on freedom of expression and dissent[16]. When individuals are aware of being constantly monitored, they may feel reluctant to express their opinions or engage in activities that challenge the status quo. This self-censorship can hinder social progress and democratic discourse, stifling innovation and the exchange of ideas.

To strike a balance between security and privacy, exploring alternatives to invasive surveillance is crucial. Privacy-enhancing technologies[17], such as encryption and decentralized systems, can give individuals greater control over their data while allowing legitimate law enforcement activities. Solid legal frameworks and independent oversight mechanisms can ensure surveillance practices are conducted within ethical boundaries and subject to checks and balances.

Moreover, engaging in an open and inclusive public debate about the ethical implications of surveillance is essential. This debate should involve various stakeholders, including policymakers, legal experts, technologists, human rights advocates, and the general public. By fostering a dialogue encompassing diverse perspectives, we can ensure that decisions regarding surveillance practices are made democratically and transparently.

---

[15] French, M., & Smith, G. J. D. (2016). Surveillance and embodiment. *Body & Society*, *22*(2), 3–27. https://doi.org/10.1177/1357034x16643169

[16] Esen, B., & Gumuscu, S. (2016). Rising competitive authoritarianism in Turkey. *Third World Quarterly*, *37*(9), 1581–1606. https://doi.org/10.1080/01436597.2015.1135732

[17] Adams, C. (2021). *Introduction to privacy enhancing technologies: A Classification-Based Approach to Understanding PETs*. Springer.

As explored earlier in this chapter, the international dimension of surveillance ethics is particularly problematic. In an increasingly interconnected world, surveillance practices can have global implications, raising questions about jurisdiction, data sharing, and the protection of human rights across borders. Establishing international norms and agreements that address these issues and ensuring that surveillance practices adhere to universally recognized ethical standards is necessary.

Furthermore, education and awareness are crucial in shaping public attitudes towards surveillance. Educating individuals about their rights, the implications of surveillance, and the potential risks and benefits associated with different technologies is essential. By promoting digital literacy and fostering a critical understanding of surveillance practices, individuals can make informed choices and actively participate in shaping policies that govern surveillance technologies.

The ethics of surveillance[18] are complex and multifaceted, encompassing issues of transparency, accountability, consent, and the balance between security and privacy. The widespread deployment of surveillance technologies raises concerns about individual rights and potential abuse. Therefore, it is imperative to approach surveillance critically, ensuring that ethical considerations are at the forefront of policy decisions and implementation. By promoting transparency, accountability, and informed consent, we can balance the legitimate needs for security and protecting individual rights. Through open and inclusive discussions, international cooperation, and education, we can navigate the ethical challenges posed by surveillance and build a society that upholds fundamental values while addressing the evolving threats of the modern world.

---

[18] Macnish, K. (2017). *The ethics of surveillance: An Introduction*. Routledge.

Chapter 4
The Impact of Surveillance on privacy

"The right to privacy is one of the cornerstones of our democracy."

Edward Snowden

In the age of mass surveillance, privacy has become a precious commodity that is increasingly under threat. This chapter explores the multifaceted impact of surveillance on privacy, considering the erosion of privacy rights, the psychological effects on individuals, and the legal and regulatory framework that governs privacy and surveillance. Through real-world examples, we uncover the profound implications of surveillance on individuals and society.

The erosion of privacy in the age of mass surveillance

Mass surveillance has significantly eroded privacy as personal data is collected, stored, and analyzed unprecedentedly. Governments, corporations, and other entities leverage sophisticated technologies to gather vast data about individuals' activities, preferences, and behavior. This includes monitoring digital communications, tracking online behavior, and conducting physical surveillance through camera networks.

One example of the erosion of privacy is the case of Edward Snowden and the revelations surrounding the surveillance programs in the United States. Edward Snowden, a former intelligence contractor, rose to prominence in 2013 when he exposed the massive surveillance programs conducted by the National Security Agency (NSA). Through his whistleblowing efforts, Snowden released a trove of classified documents that revealed the extent of global surveillance, sparking an international debate on privacy, government surveillance, and the implications of his actions.

Snowden's leaked documents exposed several highly classified surveillance programs operated. In the previous chapter, we discussed the five eyes alliance, but there were other programs[19]. The most significant revelation was the PRISM program, which involved collecting massive amounts of user data from major tech companies like Google, Facebook, Microsoft, and Apple. The leaked documents also shed light on other programs, including XKeyscore, Boundless

---

[19] https://www.bbc.com/news/world-us-canada-23123964

Informant, and Tempora, which involved the monitoring and collecting of global communications, internet traffic, and metadata[20].

These revelations sparked widespread public concern and ignited a global conversation about the balance between national security and privacy rights. Snowden's leaks provided concrete evidence of the extent to which governments were engaged in mass surveillance, raising questions about these programs' legality, proportionality, and transparency. His disclosures fueled discussions about the erosion of privacy rights and the potential abuse of surveillance powers.

Snowden's decision to leak classified documents had significant personal implications. Faced with prosecution under the Espionage Act, he fled the United States and sought asylum in Russia. Snowden's actions resulted in a life in exile, separated from his family and unable to return home. He remains a controversial figure, with supporters viewing him as a whistleblower who exposed government overreach, while others see him as a traitor who compromised national security.

Snowden's memoir[21], "Permanent Record," provides a detailed account of his motivations and the events that led to his decision to become a whistleblower. In the book, Snowden discusses his experiences working within the intelligence community and his growing disillusionment with the surveillance programs he encountered. The memoir offers insights into the personal and ethical considerations that guided his actions and sheds light on the inner workings of the surveillance apparatus he exposed.

The release of Snowden's documents prompted increased scrutiny of surveillance programs by governments, civil society organizations, and the media. Journalists such as Glenn Greenwald[22], Laura Poitras[23], and Barton Gellman worked closely with Snowden to analyze and report on the leaked documents. The resulting articles and investigative reports shed light on the surveillance practices of various governments worldwide, sparking public outrage and calling for transparency and accountability.

---

[20] https://www.vox.com/2015/6/1/18093692/nsa-and-ed-snowden

[21] Snowden, E. (2019). *Permanent record*. Metropolitan Books.

[22] Greenwald, G. (2014b). *No place to hide: Edward Snowden, the NSA and the Surveillance State*. Penguin UK

[23] Danchev, A. (2015). Troublemakers: Laura Poitras and the problem of dissent. *International Affairs*. https://doi.org/10.1111/1468-2346.12241

There have been significant policy and legal developments in the years following Snowden's revelations. For example, in the United States, the USA FREEDOM Act was enacted in 2015, which curtailed certain aspects of government surveillance and introduced reforms to enhance transparency and oversight. Additionally, the European Union implemented the General Data Protection Regulation[24] (GDPR) in 2018, strengthening data protection and privacy rights for European citizens.

Snowden's leaks inspired other whistleblowers and activists to challenge surveillance practices and advocate for privacy rights. The impact of his actions can be seen in the continued efforts of organizations like the Electronic Frontier Foundation (EFF) and the American Civil Liberties Union (ACLU) to promote digital privacy and fight against unconstitutional surveillance. These organizations and individuals influenced by Snowden's revelations continue to challenge the legality and scope of surveillance programs through legal actions, public advocacy, and educational initiatives.

However, it is essential to note that Snowden's actions and the subsequent fallout remain controversial[25]. Critics argue that his leaks endangered national security and compromised intelligence operations, while proponents argue that his disclosures were necessary to expose the overreach of surveillance programs and protect individual privacy rights. The debate surrounding Snowden's actions underscores the complexities of balancing security concerns with civil liberties and highlights the ongoing tensions between the need for secrecy and the importance of transparency in a democratic society[26].

An increasingly interconnected and monitored world

The proliferation of social media platforms and the prevalence of online tracking have amplified privacy concerns[27]. Companies like Facebook and Google collect vast amounts of personal data, including user preferences, search history, and location information, to target advertising and shape user experiences. This data-driven business model blurs the boundaries between private and public spaces, leaving individuals vulnerable to invasive surveillance practices.

---

[24] Voigt, P., & Von Dem Bussche, A. (2017). The EU General Data Protection Regulation (GDPR). In *Springer eBooks*. https://doi.org/10.1007/978-3-319-57959-7

[25] https://www.theatlantic.com/ideas/archive/2023/06/edward-snowden-nsa-mass-surveillance/674315/

[26] https://www.npr.org/2014/02/18/279151014/debate-was-edward-snowden-justified

[27] Bakir, V., & McStay, A. (2017). Fake News and The Economy of Emotions. *Digital Journalism*, 6(2), 154–175. https://doi.org/10.1080/21670811.2017.1345645

The Cambridge analytica scandal: breach of trust and data manipulation

The Cambridge Analytica scandal[28] was a watershed moment that shook the world's perception of data privacy and highlighted the potential dangers of unscrupulous data harvesting and manipulation. This scandal, which unfolded in early 2018, revealed how personal data from millions of Facebook users was improperly obtained and exploited for targeted political advertising purposes. At the heart of the scandal was Cambridge Analytica, a now-defunct British political consulting firm, and its connection to harvesting Facebook user data. The firm, led by CEO Alexander Nix, claimed to possess sophisticated data analysis techniques that could sway public opinion and influence election outcomes. It attracted attention due to its involvement in various high-profile political campaigns, including those of Donald Trump and the Brexit referendum.

The scandal was first exposed by The Guardian newspaper and The New York Times in March 2018, drawing on the investigative efforts of Carole Cadwalladr, a journalist at The Guardian, and a team of reporters, including Matthew Rosenberg, Nicholas Confessore, and Cecilia Kang[29]. Their reporting shed light on the unethical practices employed by Cambridge Analytica and its ties to the global political landscape.

The primary method through which Cambridge Analytica obtained personal data was a third-party app called "This Is Your Digital Life"[30]. Data scientist Aleksandr Kogan and Global Science Research the app in 2013. In addition to creating psychological profiles for users, the app collected personal data from their friends' profiles via Facebook's Open Graph platform. A total of 87 million Facebook profiles were analyzed in the app. Cambridge Analytica utilized this data to provide analytical support to the 2016 presidential campaigns of Ted Cruz and Donald Trump. The company was also accused of interfering in the Brexit referendum in the aftermath of the Cambridge Analytica scandal. However, the official investigation found that the company's involvement was limited to some initial inquiries, with no significant breaches taking place[31]. The data misuse was brought to light in 2018 by Christopher Wylie[32], a former employee of

---

[28] Sesay, A. (2021). *Framing the Cambridge Analytica-Facebook scandal in U.S. and U.K. newspapers: A Quantitative Content Analysis.*

[29] https://www.wired.com/story/wired-facebook-cambridge-analytica-coverage/

[30] https://en.wikipedia.org/wiki/Facebook%E2%80%93Cambridge_Analytica_data_scandal

[31] https://www.bbc.com/news/uk-politics-54457407

[32] https://en.wikipedia.org/wiki/Christopher_Wylie

Cambridge Analytica, during interviews with The Guardian[33] and The New York Times[34]. Subsequently, Facebook apologized for their role in the data harvesting, and CEO Mark Zuckerberg testified in front of Congress[35]. In July 2019, Facebook was fined $5 billion by the Federal Trade Commission for privacy violations[36]. Furthermore, in October 2019, Facebook agreed to pay a £500,000 fine to the UK Information Commissioner's Office[37] for exposing its users' data to a "serious risk of harm". As a result of these events, Cambridge Analytica filed for Chapter 7 bankruptcy in May 2018[38].

The revelations surrounding the scandal triggered widespread public outrage and led to calls for increased scrutiny of data privacy practices. It exposed the vulnerabilities in the Facebook platform and raised concerns about the misuse of personal data in targeted advertising and political campaigns[39]. The scandal also spurred investigations by regulatory bodies and lawmakers, including the U.S. Federal Trade Commission (FTC) and the U.K. Information Commissioner's Office (ICO)[40].

The investigative work of Carole Cadwalladr[41] and The Guardian was pivotal in uncovering the Cambridge Analytica scandal. Cadwalladr's in-depth reporting shed light on the inner workings of the firm and its involvement in political campaigns, ultimately leading to increased public awareness and scrutiny of the issue. Her reporting, which earned her the prestigious Orwell Prize for Journalism, demonstrated the power of investigative journalism in holding powerful entities accountable. Furthermore, the documentary "The Great Hack," directed by Karim Amer and Jehane Noujaim, provided a visual narrative of the scandal[42]. The story is of whistleblower

---

[33] https://www.theguardian.com/news/2018/mar/17/cambridge-analytica-facebook-influence-us-election

[34] https://www.nytimes.com/2018/04/04/us/politics/cambridge-analytica-scandal-fallout.html

[35] https://www.cbc.ca/news/science/facebook-zuckerberg-congress-election-1.4612495

[36] https://www.reuters.com/article/technology/facebook-to-pay-record-5-billion-us-fine-over-privacy-faces-antitrust-probe-idUSKCN1UJ1L9/

[37] https://www.bbc.com/news/technology-50234141

[38] https://www.nytimes.com/2018/05/02/us/politics/cambridge-analytica-shut-down.html

[39] Margetts, H. (2018). 9. Rethinking Democracy with Social Media. *The Political Quarterly*, *90*, 107–123. https://doi.org/10.1111/1467-923x.12574

[40] https://ico.org.uk/about-the-ico/media-centre/news-and-blogs/2022/09/action-taken-against-seven-organisations-who-failed-in-their-duty-to-respond-to-information-access-requests/

[41] Zarsky, T. (2019). Privacy and manipulation. *Theoretical Inquiries in Law*, *20*(1), 157–188. https://doi.org/10.1515/til-2019-0006

[42] https://www.slideshare.net/slideshow/the-great-hack-review-how-your-data-became-a-commodity/157521995

Christopher Wylie, a former employee of Cambridge Analytica, who exposed the company's data practices. "The Great Hack" catalyzed public discourse and amplified the understanding of the scandal's implications for democracy, data privacy, and digital manipulation.

The Cambridge Analytica scandal highlighted the urgent need for more robust data protection regulations and greater accountability from tech giants like Facebook. It prompted a reevaluation of privacy policies and data-sharing practices, leading to significant changes in the regulatory landscape. In the United States, the scandal resulted in the implementation of the California Consumer Privacy Act (CCPA)[43] and discussions around federal privacy legislation. In Europe, it played a role in developing and implementing the General Data Protection Regulation (GDPR), a comprehensive data protection framework aimed at safeguarding individuals' privacy rights. The scandal also had profound implications for public trust in technology companies and their handling of personal data. It exposed the vast power asymmetry between users and data-driven corporations and fueled discussions around data ownership, consent, and the ethical responsibilities of tech companies. Academics and experts like Shoshana Zuboff, have examined the ethical and societal implications of the Cambridge Analytica scandal. Zuboff's work explores how the commodification of personal data has given rise to surveillance capitalism, where individuals' privacy is exploited for economic gain, raising concerns about the erosion of autonomy and democratic processes.

The fallout from the Cambridge Analytica scandal extended beyond politics, underscoring the need for individuals to be more vigilant about their online privacy and data security[44]. Users became more aware of the risks of sharing personal information online and the potential for misusing it. The scandal prompted many to reassess their online behaviors, increasing the adoption of privacy-enhancing tools and practices.

In response to the scandal, Facebook faced significant backlash and was compelled to change its data policies and practices. The company tightened its third-party data access, implemented more stringent user consent processes, and introduced measures to increase transparency and accountability. However, the incident served as a wake-up call for the broader tech industry and highlighted the need for more robust data protection regulations and ethical standards.

The Cambridge Analytica scandal also prompted a broader societal conversation about the role of social media platforms in democracy and elections[45]. It raised concerns about the potential

---

[43] https://www.sciencedirect.com/science/article/abs/pii/S0736585320300903

[44] https://knowledge.wharton.upenn.edu/podcast/knowledge-at-wharton-podcast/fallout-cambridge-analytica/

[45] https://knowledge.wharton.upenn.edu/podcast/knowledge-at-wharton-podcast/fallout-cambridge-analytica/

manipulation of public opinion through targeted advertising and micro-targeting techniques[46]. The scandal emphasized safeguarding democratic processes and protecting them from undue influence and manipulation.

The Cambridge Analytica scandal exposed the dangers of unscrupulous data harvesting and manipulation. The investigative efforts of journalists like Carole Cadwalladr and documentaries like "The Great Hack" played a crucial role in uncovering the truth and raising public awareness. The scandal sparked discussions about data privacy, ethical practices, and the need for robust regulations to protect individuals' rights. It underscored the power imbalance between users and tech companies and highlighted the need for greater transparency, accountability, and informed consent. The implications of the Cambridge Analytica scandal continue to shape the discourse around data privacy, digital manipulation, and the role of technology in society, prompting individuals, policymakers, and tech companies to reevaluate their approaches to data protection and ethical practices.

The psychological effects of constant surveillance on individuals

Constant surveillance has profound psychological effects on individuals,[47] often resulting in heightened anxiety, stress, and paranoia. The knowledge that one's actions and communications are monitored creates a pervasive sense of being observed and judged, leading to self-censorship and inhibiting self-expression and personal freedom. The concept of the Panopticon, introduced by philosopher Jeremy Bentham in the late 18th century, provides a valuable framework for understanding the psychological impact of constant surveillance. In the Panopticon model, a centrally controlled prison design, inmates are under the constant threat of observation, even though they may not be directly monitored at all times. The mere possibility of being watched induces a state of self-consciousness, prompting individuals to modify their behavior and conform to societal norms, even without explicit surveillance[48]. Dr Michel Foucault, a prominent French philosopher and social theorist[49], further explored the psychological implications of the Panopticon in his seminal work "Discipline and Punish The Birth of the Prison"[50] Foucault argued that the Panopticon's design and the perpetual state of potential observation exert power that disciplines individuals, moulding them into compliant

[46] https://time.com/5197255/facebook-cambridge-analytica-donald-trump-ads-data/

[47] Steen, M., & Thomas, M. (2015). *Mental health across the lifespan: A Handbook.* Routledge

[48] https://www.sciencedirect.com/science/article/pii/S1053810019301242

[49] https://www.britannica.com/biography/Michel-Foucault

[50] https://www.amazon.com/Discipline-Punish-Prison-Michel-Foucault/dp/0679752552

and self-regulating subjects. This disciplinary power becomes internalized, leading individuals to regulate their behavior even when surveillance is absent.

Numerous studies and research have analytically examined the psychological effects of surveillance on individuals[51]. In their study "The Influence of Surveillance Cameras on Unethical Behavior: A Study of Moderating Factors"[52] Stürmer, Snyder, and Kropp (2006) found that surveillance cameras can significantly impact individuals' behavior. The participants were more likely to comply with ethical standards when they believed they were under surveillance, suggesting a self-regulatory effect induced by surveillance.

In another study titled "The Effects of Surveillance Cameras and Locus of Control on Privacy Attitudes," Stutzman and Kramer (2010) explored the psychological effects of surveillance cameras on individuals' attitudes towards privacy[53]. The results indicated that individuals exposed to surveillance cameras reported higher levels of concern regarding their privacy and personal autonomy, suggesting that surveillance impacts individuals' psychological well-being.

The work of Dr Shoshana Zuboff, a scholar and author of "The Age of Surveillance Capitalism: The Fight for a Human Future at the New Frontier of Power," provides further insights into the psychological impact of constant surveillance. Zuboff argues that surveillance capitalism, driven by the commodification of personal data, not only erodes privacy but also undermines individuals' autonomy, leading to a state of "instrumentation power." This power asymmetry, where individuals are constantly monitored and manipulated for economic gain, engenders feelings of powerlessness, anxiety, and diminished agency.

Furthermore, the psychological effects of surveillance extend beyond traditional forms of surveillance to encompass online tracking and digital monitoring. Research by Dr Sarah Roberts, author of "Behind the Screen: Content Moderation in the Shadows of Social Media"[54] explores the toll of content moderation, a form of digital surveillance, on the psychological well-being of workers. The constant exposure to disturbing and harmful content places these workers under immense psychological strain, leading to stress, depression, and post-traumatic stress disorder (PTSD).

---

[51] https://www.harvardmagazine.com/2016/12/the-watchers

[52] https://www.frontiersin.org/journals/psychology/articles/10.3389/fpsyg.2018.01937/full

[53] Weckert, J. (2005). *Electronic monitoring in the workplace: Controversies and Solutions*. IGI Global.

[54] https://www.amazon.com/Behind-Screen-Content-Moderation-Shadows/dp/0300235887

Constant surveillance exerts profound psychological effects on individuals, causing heightened anxiety, stress, and paranoia. The Panopticon concept, developed by Jeremy Bentham and expounded upon by scholars like Michel Foucault, provides a valuable framework for understanding the psychological impact of being under constant observation. Numerous studies, such as those by Stürmer, Snyder, Kropp and Stutzman and Kramer, reinforce that surveillance alters individuals' behavior and attitudes, inducing self-regulation and privacy concerns. The works of scholars like Shoshana Zuboff and Sarah Roberts shed light on the broader psychological implications of surveillance capitalism and digital monitoring, illustrating how constant surveillance erodes autonomy, agency, and psychological well-being.

It is essential to recognize that the psychological effects of constant surveillance are not limited to specific contexts or individuals, and they also have societal implications[55]. When individuals feel constantly monitored and judged, it can have an eroding effect on free speech and creativity. People may hesitate to express themselves authentically, stifling innovation and the exchange of ideas. This phenomenon, known as the "chilling effect"[56], has been observed in various domains, including online communication platforms and public spaces.

The impact of constant surveillance on mental health cannot be overlooked. Studies have shown that individuals subjected to constant surveillance experience higher stress, anxiety, and paranoia levels. This psychological burden can lead to decreased productivity, impaired decision-making, and an overall decline in well-being. Additionally, the constant fear of being watched can contribute to a culture of self-censorship and conformity, stifling individuality and diversity of thought.

Real-world examples highlight the detrimental effects of constant surveillance on individuals and society. Moreover, the growing prevalence of social media platforms and online tracking mechanisms has raised concerns about the erosion of privacy and the psychological toll on individuals. The Cambridge Analytica scandal demonstrated the potential abuse of surveillance technologies and its impact on individuals' psychological well-being.

To mitigate the psychological effects of constant surveillance, there is a need for robust legal and regulatory frameworks that safeguard privacy rights, promote transparency, and ensure accountability. The works of academics like Julie E. Cohen, author of "Between Truth and Power:

---

[55] https://repository.uel.ac.uk/download/
031c46357cb4584f66b1c87df14152efe5a90023409429f1d3cb879d6d4be49f/221578/
Experiencing%20the%20'surveillance%20society'%20%28as%20appeared%29.pdf

[56] https://pen.org/research-resources/chilling-effects/

The Legal Constructions of Informational Capitalism"[57], explore the role of law and policy in protecting individual autonomy and privacy in the face of pervasive surveillance practices. Constant surveillance has profound psychological effects on individuals, including heightened anxiety, stress, and paranoia. The Panopticon concept[58] research studies, and the works of scholars provide insights into the psychological impact of being constantly monitored and its implications for behavior, self-expression, and well-being. Real-world examples, such as the Snowden revelations and the Cambridge Analytica scandal, highlight the importance of addressing the psychological consequences of constant surveillance. By establishing strong legal protections, promoting transparency, and fostering a culture that values privacy, societies can mitigate the adverse psychological effects of constant surveillance and safeguard individual autonomy and well-being[59].

Studies have also demonstrated the psychological on individuals that are aware of being monitored online . These people usually exhibit self-censorship, refraining from expressing dissenting opinions or engaging in controversial discussions. This chilling effect on freedom of expression undermines democratic discourse and stifles the diversity of ideas and opinions.

The legal and regulatory framework surrounding privacy and surveillance

The legal and regulatory framework surrounding privacy and surveillance plays a crucial role in protecting individuals' rights and limiting the use of surveillance. Laws and regulations vary across countries, but many jurisdictions recognize the importance of privacy as a fundamental human right.

The General Data Protection Regulation (GDPR)[60] implemented in the European Union is one example of comprehensive privacy legislation. It grants individuals control over personal data and obligates organizations to handle data responsibly. The GDPR has significant implications for surveillance practices, requiring transparency, consent, and data protection measures. The GDPR signals Europe's commitment to data privacy and security at a time when more people trust cloud services with their data, and data breaches are everyday. The GDPR is large, far-reaching, and fairly light on specifics, making GDPR compliance a daunting prospect, especially for small and medium-sized enterprises (SMEs).

---

[57] https://www.amazon.com/Between-Truth-Power-Constructions-Informational/dp/0190246693

[58] https://en.wikipedia.org/wiki/Panopticon

[59] https://www.cambridge.org/core/books/digital-constitutionalism-in-europe/digital-constitutionalism-privacy-and-data-protection/E1725A06254D721E8E5D1D6B461CFAA2

[60] https://gdpr-info.eu/

The GDPR has a long history[61]. Among the rights guaranteed by the 1950 European Convention on Human Rights[62] is the right to privacy, which states, "Everyone has the right to respect his personal and family life, his home, and his correspondence." This right has been protected by legislation by the European Union based on this principle. In 1995, the EU passed the precursor to the GDPR, named the European Data Protection Directive[63], which set the minimum standards for data privacy and security, based on which each member state drafted its own legislation to implement it. The EU recognized the need for modern protections as technology progressed and the Internet was developed and grew into common use. By 1994, the Internet had already begun to transform into a data hoover. In 2000, online banking became the norm across much of Europe[64]. In 2006, Facebook opened to the public. In 2011, a Google user sued the company for scanning her emails. In the month following, the EU's data protection authority called for a comprehensive approach to protecting personal data and began updating the 1995 directive. As of May 25, 2018, all organizations were required to comply with GDPR, which was passed by the European Parliament in 2016.

The primary reason for the development of safe guards in privacy in Europe as apposed to elsewhere is the history of Europe itself. Privacy has been violated in Europe for many years. The Nazi regime used highly sensitive personal data from local population registers to round up Jews during World War II, with horrendous consequences. As surveillance and repression of dissent became perfected in communist East Germany, the combined secret police and intelligence agency Stasi engulfed every aspect of civilian life. In light of this backdrop, it is not surprising that Europe has made great strides in ensuring people's privacy.

In contrast, U.S. legislation does not protect consumer privacy interests adequately. Before the GDPR came into effect on May 25, 2018, the U.S. Congress introduced the Clarifying Lawful Overseas Use of Data (CLOUD) Act on March 23, 2018[65]. This act, rather than aligning with the GDPR, actually supersedes it, setting the stage for a potential conflict in data privacy laws[66]. If there is a suspicion of a crime, U.S. law enforcement officials can obtain personal information

[61] https://www.edps.europa.eu/data-protection/data-protection/legislation/history-general-data-protection-regulation_en

[62] https://en.wikipedia.org/wiki/European_Convention_on_Human_Rights

[63] https://www.digitalguardian.com/blog/what-data-protection-directive-predecessor-gdpr

[64] https://www.researchgate.net/publication/362404964_Consumer_Adoption_of_Digital-only_Banking_in_Europe_-_An_Application_of_the_Extended_Technology_Acceptance_Model

[65] https://en.wikipedia.org/wiki/CLOUD_Act

[66] https://www.activemind.legal/guides/us-cloud-act/

from US-based technology companies through a warrant or court order, regardless of where the data is located, under the CLOUD Act. As a result, service providers must disclose any information about their customers they possess, regardless of whether that information is located inside or outside of the United States. Therefore, US authorities could access and process large amounts of EU citizens' personal data. From the U.S. perspective, the goal is to ensure that U.S. companies adhere to U.S. laws, regardless of where they have their servers and whose data is stored, and to expedite data exchanges for law enforcement purposes. In contrast, the CLOUD Act circumvents foreign data protection rules, leaving businesses in a conflicted position of complying with U.S. law enforcement requests while ensuring personal data protection.

For a U.S.-based software company or IT service provider, it's crucial to ensure that all data stored on foreign servers is accessible to authorities, as mandated by US federal law[67]. This not only shields U.S. service providers from the obligation to inform customers about data requests but also raises concerns about the potential transfer of data to the U.S. government, which can then distribute it as it deems fit, potentially impacting European companies and their data privacy.

How did this come about? It has to do with the influence of large tech companies in the US and their dominant role in economic governance and regulation. Regarding economic governance, the EU has significant structural differences from the U.S. The centre of gravity in the EU is Brussels, where many politicians meet to work and advance together. Economically, the West Coast of the U.S. and Silicon Valley, in particular, are at the centre of gravity. Because big tech companies can provide so much personal data to U.S. government intelligence agencies, it's unsurprising that they have a long history of close cooperation with them.

Hence, Big tech companies have a significant stake in ensuring that online privacy regulations in the United States are robust. They also need to that their business models remain open. This is not only a matter of economic interest but also a strategic move, as control of knowledge can translate into power in the digital landscape.

One lobbying group representing internet companies is seeking a federal privacy law that preempts more state regulations like the California Consumer Privacy Act (CCPA), making real progress. As a result of its ideal federal privacy law, companies would be allowed to continue doing business as usual while the CCPA would be undermined. Additionally, other states could not raise the bar even higher. A restriction on consumer data could also set U.S. tech companies

---

[67] https://legal.thomsonreuters.com/en/insights/articles/understanding-data-privacy-and-cloud-computing

back significantly against Chinese companies in areas such as artificial intelligence, the argument goes.

Unlike the typical mindset in Europe, many Americans are less sensitive to privacy issues[68]. Most Americans believe that tracking their online behavior is in their best interest or a price to pay for free products or discounts. Despite Edward Snowden revealing how vastly expanded the government's spying powers were after Congress passed the Patriot Act legislation, only half of Americans said they disagreed with the government's actions.

While Americans struggle to protect their digital privacy, there are some steps they can take to do so. For better data protection, it is best to use technology developed by EU-headquartered companies and thinking about how to do your daily online activities more privately, such as switching to private search. More on that later.

The facts speak for themselves.   There are 14 European countries that demonstrate the highest commitment to digital privacy in the internet privacy rankings (the U.S. ranks 18th)[69].

Progress in privacy in the United States has largely been through the courts. Landmark legal cases have challenged the legality and scope of surveillance. The 2013 United States Supreme Court ruling in the case of United States v. Jones established that prolonged GPS tracking of an individual's vehicle without a warrant violated the Fourth Amendment[70]. Such cases highlight the ongoing struggle between privacy rights and surveillance practices, emphasizing the need for clear legal boundaries and judicial oversight.

The emergence of privacy-enhancing technologies (PETs) has also played a significant role in shaping the legal and regulatory landscape. PETs aim to protect individuals' privacy by offering encryption, anonymization, and other tools that safeguard personal data from unwarranted surveillance. For instance, end-to-end encryption protocols, such as those employed by messaging apps like Signal and WhatsApp, ensure that only the intended recipients can access the content of communications, providing a layer of privacy in an increasingly monitored digital world.

Nevertheless, ongoing debates exist regarding the appropriate balance between privacy and national security. Critics argue that excessive surveillance measures encroach upon individuals'

[68] https://www.nbcnews.com/id/wbna15221111

[69] https://online.stevens.edu/info/countries-ranked-by-internet-privacy/

[70] https://en.wikipedia.org/wiki/United_States_v._Jones_(2012)

privacy rights and threaten civil liberties. On the other hand, proponents contend that surveillance is necessary to combat crime, terrorism, and other threats to public safety. Striking the right balance between these competing interests remains a complex challenge for lawmakers and policymakers worldwide.

The impact of surveillance on privacy is far-reaching, encompassing the erosion of privacy rights, psychological effects on individuals, and the legal and regulatory framework that seeks to govern surveillance practices. Real-world examples, such as the revelations of Edward Snowden and the prevalence of online tracking, underscore the profound implications of surveillance in the modern world.

It is essential to recognize the significance of privacy as a fundamental human right and to establish robust legal frameworks that protect individuals' privacy while allowing for necessary surveillance activities. Achieving the right balance between security concerns and privacy rights requires ongoing dialogue, public engagement, and the involvement of stakeholders from various sectors.

As technology advances and surveillance capabilities evolve, ensuring that privacy remains a central consideration in policy discussions is imperative. By promoting transparency, accountability, and the responsible use of surveillance, societies can navigate the complexities of the . while safeguarding individual autonomy, self-determination, and the right to privacy.

Chapter 5
The consequences of surveillance

"The ultimate tragedy is not the oppression and cruelty by the bad people but the silence over that by the good people."

Martin Luther King Jr.

Mass surveillance has unintended consequences in diverse arenas of social trust, democratic values, individual behavior, free speech, and dissent.

This chapter examines the consequences of these repercussions concerning individuals and the broader societal fabric, shedding light on these profound consequences as a result of these repercussions. It examines the effects of mass surveillance on social trust, the chilling effect on free speech and dissent, and the potential for abuse and misuse of surveillance technologies.

Academic writings on the mass surveillance of society

There is a growing volume of academic and mass media work on the impact of mass surveillance. Mass surveillance will inevitably have many unintended consequences that go far beyond the stated purposes for which it was intended. As a result, trust is eroded between people in society and one of the consequences is the erosion of trust between individuals. Whenever people become aware that their activities, communications, and private lives are constantly being monitored, they immediately become filled with suspicion and skepticism that permeates every aspect of their daily lives[71]. Undoubtedly, the erosion of trust has wide-ranging implications for societal cohesion and the functioning of democratic systems since it undermines the core values of cooperation and collective action that are the basis of democratic societies[72].

Mass surveillance is also capable of undermining democratic values[73]. Constant observation can lead to self-censorship and conformity due to the feeling that one is being monitored. Those

---

[71] https://www.researchgate.net/publication/
380889515_Surveillance_Omnipotence_A_Thought_Experiment_on_Total_Global_Surveillance

[72] https://assets.publishing.service.gov.uk/media/65fdbfd265ca2ffef17da79c/The_Khan_review.pdf

[73] https://academic.oup.com/jhrp/article/16/1/397/7234270

who fear retribution or negative consequences may be reluctant to express dissenting views or engage in open discussions on controversial topics. Self-censorship narrows the public sphere, stifles diversity, and undermines democratic participation, thus undermining the essence of democracy.

Mass surveillance curtails free speech and dissent, creating a climate of fear and self-censorship that hampers the open exchange of ideas, inhibits critical discourse, and undermines democratic governance[74]. The awareness of constant monitoring and the potential consequences of expressing dissenting views or engaging in political activism restricts individuals from exercising their right to free speech[75]. This effect has been extensively studied and supported by numerous authors, scholars, and academics who have shed light on its societal implications.

In her book "Hate Crimes in Cyberspace"[76], Danielle Keats Citron[77] explores the significant effect of surveillance on free speech and expression. She discusses how individuals, especially marginalized groups, may hesitate to voice their opinions online due to the fear of surveillance targeting, online harassment, or legal repercussions. This climate of self-censorship restricts the diversity of voices and limits the exploration of unconventional or controversial ideas, hindering societal progress.

Sociologist Zeynep Tufekci[78], in her book "Twitter and Tear Gas: The Power and Fragility of Networked Protest"[79], explores the impact of surveillance on activism and dissent. Tufekci argues that surveillance acts as a form of social control, deterring individuals from participating in political activism. The fear of being monitored and targeted undermines the collective power of social movements and weakens the ability to challenge prevailing narratives and policies.

In his book "No Place to Hide: Edward Snowden, the NSA, and the U.S. Surveillance State"[80], legal scholar and activist Glenn Greenwald highlights how the pervasive surveillance apparatus

---

[74] https://theintercept.com/2016/04/28/new-study-shows-mass-surveillance-breeds-meekness-fear-and-self-censorship/

[75] https://www.ncbi.nlm.nih.gov/pmc/articles/PMC10008147/

[76] https://www.hup.harvard.edu/books/9780674659902

[77] https://www.law.virginia.edu/faculty/profile/uqg7tt/2964150

[78] https://sociology.princeton.edu/people/zeynep-tufekci

[79] https://yalebooks.yale.edu/book/9780300234176/twitter-and-tear-gas/

[80] https://us.macmillan.com/books/9781250062581/noplacetohide

undermines the necessary conditions for democratic societies. He emphasizes that the erosion of privacy and the subduing effect on free speech impede the ability of individuals to engage in meaningful political discourse and challenge the status quo.

Academic research widely supports the notion that mass surveillance has a eroding effect on the desire to engage in free speech and dissent[81]. A study[82] by Elizabeth Stoycheff, a professor of communication at Wayne State University[83], found that the perception of being under surveillance leads to self-censorship and reduced political expression[84]. The fear of surveillance and its potential consequences discourage individuals from engaging in open discussions, sharing controversial opinions, or participating in political activism. The consequences of the this extend beyond individual liberty. It weakens democratic governance and threatens social stability by limiting the avenues through which societal problems can be identified and addressed. By silencing dissenting voices, mass surveillance curtails the checks and balances that are vital for a healthy democracy. The absence of critical discourse inhibits the ability to challenge prevailing narratives, question authority, and hold those in power accountable. Moreover, the suppression of free speech and dissent hinders innovation, creativity, and societal progress. Unconventional or controversial ideas often challenge existing norms and pave the way for new solutions to societal problems. When individuals fear surveillance and potential repercussions, they are less likely to explore alternative perspectives or challenge the status quo[85]. This stifles intellectual diversity and inhibits the free flow of ideas necessary for societal advancement.

Authors who have explored the potential for abuse and misuse of surveillance technology

The potential for abuse and misuse of surveillance technology raises serious concerns about civil liberties, human rights, and the emergence of authoritarian practices. Numerous authors and academics have shed light on these issues, emphasizing the risks posed to individuals and society.

---

[81] https://unesdoc.unesco.org/ark:/48223/pf0000246610

[82] https://www.washingtonpost.com/news/the-switch/wp/2016/03/28/mass-surveillance-silences-minority-opinions-according-to-study/

[83] https://scholar.google.com/citations?user=7cJhUEkAAAAJ&hl=en

[84] https://journals.sagepub.com/doi/10.1177/1077699016630255

[85] https://www.harvardmagazine.com/2016/12/the-watchers

Returning to Shoshana Zuboff, author of "The Age of Surveillance Capitalism"[86], She delves into the intricate relationship between corporations and surveillance, shedding light on the alarming practices of extracting and monetizing personal data without individuals' consent or awareness.

Zuboff's exploration of surveillance capitalism unveils the transformation of surveillance from a mere means of observation to a pervasive system that commodifies personal information for profit. She emphasizes that data has become a valuable resource and corporations have harnessed surveillance technology to collect and analyze vast amounts of personal data, often without individuals' explicit consent or knowledge[87].

Central to Zuboff's analysis is the concept of "instrumentarian power," which she defines as the ability of powerful entities to utilize surveillance technologies to shape and control human behavior[88]. She argues that the unregulated collection and analysis of personal information enable corporations to manipulate individuals' choices, preferences, and even their sense of self, eroding privacy and autonomy[89].

Zuboff underscores the risks that surveillance capitalism poses to democratic principles. She highlights how the vast accumulation of personal data can be leveraged to influence elections, shape public opinion, and manipulate consumer behavior. Such practices undermine the principles of transparency, accountability, and informed consent essential to democratic governance. The unregulated power wielded by corporations in surveillance capitalism raises concerns about the concentration of power and the potential for societal inequality.

Drawing on extensive research and analysis, Zuboff provides a compelling argument for the urgent need to address the abuses of surveillance technology. She calls for a new social contract that places individuals' rights to privacy, autonomy, and democratic participation at the forefront. Zuboff advocates for robust regulations and legal frameworks that protect individuals from exploiting their data promote transparency in data practices and ensure accountability for the misuse of surveillance technology.

---

[86] https://www.amazon.com/Age-Surveillance-Capitalism-Future-Frontier/dp/1610395697

[87] https://medium.com/@th3Powell/surveillance-capitalism-how-tech-companies-profit-from-your-data-61c71ce7f2f

[88] https://www.sciencedirect.com/science/article/pii/S1045235421001155

[89] https://www.nytimes.com/2021/05/21/technology/shoshana-zuboff-apple-google-privacy.html

The work of Shoshana Zuboff has garnered widespread recognition and influence[90]. Her insights into the abuses of surveillance technology have resonated with scholars, policymakers, and activists alike, sparking critical conversations and shaping the discourse surrounding the impact of surveillance capitalism[91]. Her research serves as a wake-up call, urging society to confront the profound implications of unchecked surveillance and take proactive steps to safeguard privacy, autonomy, and democratic values. Her work illuminates the exploitative practices that extract and monetize personal data without individuals' consent or awareness.

Zuboff's insights into the risks to privacy, autonomy, and democratic principles highlight the urgent need for robust regulations and a reimagining of the social contract in the face of surveillance capitalism. Her work has significantly impacted understanding of the complex relationship between technology, power, and individual rights.

Naomi Klein, a prominent academic and activist[92], has also made significant contributions to the understanding of surveillance technology and its potential for misuse by governments. In her influential book, "The Shock Doctrine: The Rise of Disaster Capitalism"[93], Klein explores the intersection of surveillance, power, and authoritarian practices. Naomi Klein studied political science and philosophy at the University of Toronto. Her academic background and extensive research contribute to the credibility and depth of her analysis of surveillance technology and its potential consequences.

Klein's research and analysis shed light on the potential for surveillance technology to be employed as a tool of control and repression by governments. She argues that in the name of security and stability, authoritarian regimes may exploit surveillance capabilities to target and suppress political dissidents, activists, and minority groups. By monitoring and surveilling these individuals and groups, governments can undermine civil liberties, curtail freedom of expression, and violate fundamental human rights. While Naomi Klein's work is widely recognized and respected, it is essential to note that she does not stand alone in her views. Other academics and researchers have also highlighted the risks associated with governments' misuse of surveillance technology.

---

[90] https://www.theguardian.com/books/2019/oct/04/shoshana-zuboff-surveillance-capitalism-assault-human-automomy-digital-privacy

[91] https://www.researchgate.net/publication/332114371_Surveillance_Capitalism_An_Interview_with_Shoshana_Zuboff

[92] https://en.wikipedia.org/wiki/Naomi_Klein

[93] https://www.amazon.com/Shock-Doctrine-Rise-Disaster-Capitalism/dp/0312427999

Likewise the work of Glenn Greenwald[94], an author and journalist with the Guardian (previously discussed), provides supporting evidence into the revelations brought forth by Edward Snowden about mass surveillance programs. Greenwald exposed the extensive reach of government surveillance and the potential for abuse in the name of national security. He echoes Klein's concerns about the erosion of civil liberties and the suppression of dissent through surveillance practices.

The implications of surveillance technology on human rights is explored in detail in "Human Rights and Digital Technology: Digital Tightrope (Global Ethics)"[95], authored by Susan Perry and Claudia Roda. The authors discuss the potential for governments to exploit surveillance capabilities to silence dissenting voices and violate individuals' rights to privacy and free speech. The work explores the intricate balance between human rights protection and technological innovation in a digital age by examining the convergence of law and regulation with rapidly evolving communications technologies. It illustrates how human rights can be used to fully frame our smart use of technology. They address issues such as user privacy online, digital pollution as a health hazard, who should be in charge of data technologies and how to maintain human autonomy in a world of interconnected things. Taking specific cases as examples, this book explores the many technological and regulatory choices citizens, states, civil society organizations, and the private sector should consider to ensure that digital technology better serves humanity. The examples explored include case studies of user privacy violations, including data breaches, where personal information is stolen from online platforms and sold on the dark web, and the unauthorized collection and use of personal data by tech companies for targeted advertising purposes. The author's work emphasises that the lack of transparency and control over how personal data is used enables third parties to threaten user privacy in the digital age.

Naomi Klein's work (previously discussed) also provides valuable support into the misuse of technological innovation by governments. Klein expands on the topics of suppression of dissent, targeting of political dissidents, and erosion of civil liberties explored by Perry and Roda. The work also resonates with other scholars such as Glenn Greenwald and Sarah Joseph.

---

94 https://www.pbs.org/wgbh/pages/frontline/government-elections-politics/united-states-of-secrets/the-frontline-interview-glenn-greenwald/

95 https://www.amazon.com/Human-Rights-Digital-Technology-Tightrope-ebook/dp/B01N9FA4KI/ref=sr_1_3?crid=25GAQO0V82YQD&dib=eyJ2IjoiMSJ9.pnRoiZlsyILH-GPW1sKbpQhwsAbJltJWTlsZQ3vNLtJRKTJ0iKJ6JsyF7ce3nCea_KxDDVX8ML0fSCQXMKuRBys5egjYJ_blf1qeCe-SrX2gyG9OD7SIGwZt8mA1FywNp8kGnWOwj6trUGDPnpZf8O7ad-Y6VqiUff7On6-z45RA--d9yEx_WYVG3kPX6jE9orq5vtI68bKX1eWmO0b1L1Yevt1CYAIgLcS3E0-2R6M.bqNTGNghVm1UfQnAG9H7Hlg3s4DXlQYjVfJU4rQygkw&dib_tag=se&keywords=technology+and+human+rights&qid=1719193507&s=digital-text&sprefix=technology+and+human+righ%2Cdigital-text%2C488&sr=1-3

Through her research and analysis, Klein contributes to the ongoing discourse on the intersection of surveillance, power, and human rights. Her work serves as a call to action, urging society to be vigilant and protect fundamental rights and freedoms in the face of increasing surveillance capabilities.

Rebecca MacKinnon[96] is another a prominent author and advocate for Internet freedom, offers valuable insights into the intersection of technology, surveillance, and human rights in her book "Consent of the Networked: The Worldwide Struggle for Internet Freedom"[97], Her work highlights the potential for abuse of surveillance tools by governments and corporations, leading to restrictions on freedoms and control over the flow of information. MacKinnon's research focuses on how surveillance technologies can be misused to curtail individual rights and stifle dissent. She explores how governments, in collaboration with powerful corporations, can exploit surveillance tools to monitor and control online activities, thereby restricting freedom of expression and limiting access to information. MacKinnon argues that such practices undermine democracy, transparency, and human rights. One of the critical themes MacKinnon emphasizes is the importance of transparency and accountability in developing and deploying surveillance technologies. She also calls for robust legal frameworks and oversight mechanisms to ensure surveillance activities are conducted within the bounds of respect for privacy and civil liberties. MacKinnon also highlights the significance of user rights, asserting that individuals should have the right to understand and control how their data is collected, used, and shared. In her book "Consent of the Networked: The Worldwide Struggle for Internet Freedom"[98], MacKinnon analyses the real-world implications of surveillance technologies on human rights and political movements. One notable example she explores is the Arab Spring uprisings, which occurred across several countries in the Middle East and North Africa in the early 2010s[99]. During the Arab Spring, citizens in countries such as Tunisia, Egypt, Libya, and Syria took to the streets to protest against oppressive regimes, demanding political reforms, freedom of expression, and social justice. As these mass protests gained momentum, governments responded by deploying various surveillance tools to monitor and suppress dissenting voices. MacKinnon highlights how these governments employed surveillance technologies to identify and target individuals organizing and participating in the protests. Monitoring internet communications, tracking social media activities, and intercepting phone calls allowed authorities to closely surveil activists and gain insights into their networks and activities. In Egypt, for example, the government of President Hosni Mubarak employed advanced

[96] https://en.wikipedia.org/wiki/Rebecca_MacKinnon

[97] https://www.amazon.com/Consent-Networked-Worldwide-Struggle-Internet/dp/0465024424

[98] https://www.amazon.com/Consent-Networked-Worldwide-Struggle-Internet/dp/0465024424

[99] https://cases.open.ubc.ca/arab-spring/

surveillance techniques to monitor online platforms and identify individuals using social media to mobilize protests[100]. They tracked keywords, monitored activists' online activities, and utilized cyber-surveillance tools to identify and locate individuals perceived as threats to the regime[101] This surveillance apparatus was used to intimidate, arrest, and silence activists, leading to a dampening effect on freedom of expression and assembly.

Similarly, President Bashar al-Assad's regime in Syria utilized surveillance technologies to suppress dissent during the uprising[102]. The government engaged in widespread monitoring of communications, including phone calls and internet activities, to identify and target activists. Such surveillance tactics were instrumental in the government's efforts to locate and arrest individuals involved in organizing protests and sharing information about the regime's human rights abuses.

These real-world examples underscore the significant impact of surveillance on political movements and dissent. By exploiting surveillance technologies, governments, in these cases, were able to gain the upper hand in their attempts to quell opposition and maintain control[103]. The ability to monitor and suppress dissenting voices limited the space for free expression and hindered the organizing capabilities of activists, ultimately impeding the progress of democratic movements. Rebecca MacKinnon's examination of these cases in "Consent of the Networked" provides concrete evidence of how surveillance technologies can be weaponized against individuals exercising their rights to free speech and peaceful assembly. Her examples demonstrate the urgent need to safeguard individual privacy, protect freedom of expression, and ensure accountability and transparency in using surveillance tools.

The case of the Arab Spring uprisings serves as a powerful illustration of how governments utilized surveillance technologies to monitor and suppress dissent[104]. Through the lens of this real-world example, Rebecca MacKinnon's work highlights the dangers of unchecked surveillance and its detrimental impact on political movements and human rights. By shining a light on these practices, MacKinnon emphasizes the need for individuals, governments, and

---

[100] https://dialnet.unirioja.es/descarga/articulo/5535753.pdf

[101] https://www.science.org/doi/10.1126/sciadv.abl8198

[102] https://www.jstor.org/stable/10.7249/j.ctt4cgd90.11?
Search=yes&resultItemClick=true&searchText=au%3A&searchText=%22Lowell%22&searchUri=%2Fopen%2Fsearch
%2F%3Ftheme%3Dopen%26amp%3Bso%3Dnew%26amp%3BQuery%3Dau%253A%2522Lowell%2522%26amp%3B
si%3D1

[103] https://www.zdnet.com/article/censorship-surveillance-and-android-phones-syrias-tech-revolution-from-the-cutting-room-floor/

[104] https://cases.open.ubc.ca/arab-spring/

technology companies to proactively address the ethical and legal implications of surveillance and work towards protecting fundamental rights and freedoms.

MacKinnon refers to the works of other academics and experts who have explored similar topics to reinforce her views. For example, she cites the research of Evgeny Morozov, a prominent surveillance critic and author of "The Net Delusion: The Dark Side of Internet Freedom"[105] who warns about the dangers of technological utopianism and the potential for surveillance to enable authoritarian control. Morozov describes how the automobile was originally thought of as a means of cleaning American cities polluted by horse manure. People have long been enamoured with the idea of technological fixes to social and political problems. According to the the press of the time, it would be "the nerve of international life", transmitting information about events, eliminating misunderstandings, and promoting peace and harmony throughout the globe[106]. The airplane would foster democracy, equality, and freedom. The invention of radio, television, and computers raised similar hopes when they purified the world of war and violence[107]. Much press was devoted to the concept that thinking machines will bring a better, happier civilization than any previously known to man[108]. It is clear from Morozov's article that Internet utopians, as attractive as they seem, are just as deluded visions and overly optimistic. It is true that Internet can and has transformed society and politics, but one needs to consider both the positives and the very real negatives.

MacKinnon's book comprehensively analyses the challenges of surveillance technologies to internet freedom and human rights. Her insights contribute to the ongoing dialogue on the need for safeguards, transparency, and accountability in deploying surveillance tools. MacKinnon urges individuals, governments, and corporations to actively protect user rights, privacy, and the free flow of information in the . by shedding light on the potential abuses and consequences of surveillance. Her work highlights the risks and potential abuses associated with surveillance tools employed by governments and corporations. Through her research, MacKinnon underscores the importance of transparency, accountability, and user rights in ensuring that surveillance technologies are developed and used responsibly while safeguarding privacy, freedom of expression, and democratic principles. Her analysis is informed by real-world examples and supported by the perspectives of other scholars and experts in the field.

---

[105] https://www.cambridge.org/core/journals/perspectives-on-politics/article/abs/net-delusion-the-dark-side-of-internet-freedom-by-evgeny-morozov-new-york-publicaffairs-2011-432p-2795/A5F6C33D2AD4F54315DA9D7BC71FE3EA

[106] https://library.oapen.org/bitstream/handle/20.500.12657/34555/410799.pdf?seq

[107] https://unesdoc.unesco.org/ark:/48223/pf0000111240

[108] https://www.weforum.org/publications/positive-ai-economic-futures/

In addition to these authors, several scholars and researchers have explored specific cases and examples of the misuse of surveillance technology. For instance, the investigative work of journalists has been hampered by surveillance, with journalists being targeted, monitored, or harassed for their reporting. The Committee to Protect Journalists (CPJ)[109], an independent nonprofit organization, has documented numerous cases of journalists facing surveillance and interference, hindering their ability to carry out their critical role in holding power accountable. The NSO Group's Pegasus[110] spyware case represents a striking example of surveillance technology being misused for political purposes. Pegasus is a highly sophisticated surveillance software developed by the Israeli NSO Group[111]. It is a powerful tool that enables remote access to mobile devices, allowing for extensive monitoring and data collection. The software can be installed on targeted devices through various means, including malicious links or exploiting vulnerabilities in operating systems. Once installed, Pegasus can access and extract a wide range of data, including call records, messages, emails, and location information, and even activate the device's camera and microphone for live surveillance[112].

Initially developed to assist law enforcement and intelligence agencies in combating terrorism and serious crimes, Pegasus was marketed as a tool for lawful interception and targeted surveillance. It was meant solely by authorized government entities to target individuals threatening national security. The software's capabilities, however, have raised concerns about potential misuse and abuse. However, in recent years, the development and sale of Pegasus by NSO Group have come under scrutiny, raising questions about accountability and the responsibility of surveillance technology companies. Critics argue that the lack of stringent controls and oversight mechanisms surrounding the use of such software has allowed for its exploitation by governments for political purposes, undermining civil liberties and human rights. Regardless, it is essential to note that NSO Group has maintained that Pegasus is intended for legitimate purposes and is only provided to vetted government entities. However, the evidence of its misuse and the potential for abuse has sparked widespread calls for stronger regulations and safeguards to prevent the unauthorized use of surveillance technology and protect individuals from unwarranted intrusions into their privacy.

However, The NSO Group's Pegasus spyware case is a significant example of the potential for surveillance technology abuse and misuse. Investigations by organizations such as Forbidden

---

[109] https://en.wikipedia.org/wiki/Committee_to_Protect_Journalists

[110] https://en.wikipedia.org/wiki/Pegasus_(spyware)

[111] https://en.wikipedia.org/wiki/NSO_Group

[112] https://greydynamics.com/decoding-pegasus-spyware-peering-into-the-underbelly-of-digital-surveillance/

Stories and Amnesty International[113]. Forbidden Stories, a Paris-based media non-profit, coordinated the Pegasus Project in partnership with Amnesty International's Security Lab, which involved more than 80 journalists from 17 media outlets in 10 countries. Numerous new Pegasus spyware attacks were confirmed by cutting-edge forensic tests conducted by the Security Lab on potentially targeted mobile devices.

As a result of the collaboration, 50,000 phone numbers of potential surveillance targets were exposed, showing how NSO Group's Pegasus spyware facilitates human rights violations around the world.

On 11 March 2022, the European Parliament voted to establish a new "committee of inquiry" to investigate abuses of Pegasus by European member states[114]. As a result of the Pegasus Project, numerous criminal cases have been brought by people who discovered their devices were targeted with the spyware, including those in France, Mexico, and India.

As a result of its "malicious cyber activity", the U.S. Department of Commerce placed NSO Group on a blocklist in November 2021. To "curb the abuse of state-sponsored spyware", Apple filed a lawsuit against NSO Group a few weeks later[115]. Amnesty International and Citizen Lab have been praised by the company for identifying cyber surveillance abuses in advance.

These cases provide real world data to support the claims and concerns of academic scholars like Shoshana Zuboff, Helen Nissenbaum, and Bruce Schneier, who have shed light on the alarming implications of unregulated surveillance practices. Helen Nissenbaum, a professor of information science and director of the Digital Life Initiative at Cornell Tech, has extensively explored the ethical implications of surveillance and the need to protect individual privacy and autonomy. Her book, "Privacy in Context: Technology, Policy, and the Integrity of Social Life"[116], comprehensively examines the challenges posed by emerging surveillance technologies.

Bruce Schneier, author of "Data and Goliath: The Hidden Battles to Collect Your Data and Control Your World"[117], It discusses the pervasive nature of surveillance and the consequences for civil liberties and democratic societies. Schneier stresses the importance of a societal dialogue to balance privacy and security, urging people to be aware of the risks associated with an unchecked expansion of surveillance tools. In order to break free from a robust digital

---

[113] https://securitylab.amnesty.org/case-study-the-pegasus-project/

[114] https://www.europarl.europa.eu/meetdocs/2014_2019/plmrep/COMMITTEES/PEGA/DV/2023/05-08/REPORTcompromises_EN.pdf

[115] https://www.nytimes.com/2022/01/28/magazine/nso-group-israel-spyware.html

[116] https://books.google.ch/books/about/Privacy_in_Context.html?id=_NN1uGn1Jd8C&redir_esc=y

[117] https://www.american.edu/sis/centers/security-technology/book-review-data-and-goliath.cfm

surveillance system that collects and controls our data, consumers must organize. Almost every internet-connected device is used to collect this data, and it includes almost every type of information imaginable.

In his book, Schneier shows how governments and companies use our data to build comprehensive profiles of everyone and create ubiquitous surveillance. He uses a variety of sources to support his argument, including legal cases, Snowden files, think tank reports, academic journals, and his own work[118].

With a wealth of knowledge and experience, Bruce Schneier approaches the topic of surveillance with authority. He is a fellow at Harvard's Berkman Center for Internet and Society and the Chief of Security Architecture at Inrupt Inc., a company dedicated to empowering users with control over their data. A respected cryptographer, computer security professional, and privacy specialist, Schneier is a best-selling author of fourteen books on security and technology. The Economist has dubbed him a "security guru", and he describes himself as a "public interest technologist".

"The World We Are Creating," "What's At Stake," and "What To Do About It" are the three parts of Data and Goliath. The first explains how our data can be gathered through any internet-connected device, then quickly sorted and analyzed with artificial intelligence. In his book, Schneier describes how that data can be used intrusively to monitor people, whether through mass surveillance programs conducted by the National Security Agency (NSA) or online manipulation by corporations. As a result of the private sector's dominance of our data, users have little control over how their data is used, sold, or stored. Consequently, it is up for sale to the highest bidder, whether it is an abusive government or a profit-motivated advertising company. This first part of the book thoroughly examines how the NSA and other government intelligence agencies, both in the United States and abroad, can infiltrate private companies to extract data. According to Schneier, the government has the right to access the data it collects and use it however they choose.

The second part of the book, titled "What's At Stake," explains how our current data collection trajectory leaves us vulnerable to abuse. A threat to political liberty and justice is what Schneier sees, which implies governments may suppress social change and political dissent, impose government censorship, or accuse users of crimes by redefining previously acceptable behaviour and, for example, creating a Facebook post criticizing a candidate's rhetoric or

---

[118] The Dawning of the Cyber-Panopticon: Navigating the Brave New World of 2030. https://www.planetpulsar.com/untitled-75/

rhetorical style. He asserts that this could have been an acceptable form of free speech before a change in law or authoritarian leadership. Still, afterward, it earns you the label of an enemy of the state. Due to the capability of aggregating data about your every move online and profiling you, Schneier argues that social media platforms pose a massive threat to political manipulation. He writes that creating a new identity and separating yourself from this online profile is very difficult. Couple this with constant surveillance, and people's freedom to do as they please is greatly diminished. Finally, he argues that the collection and exploitation of online data threaten our physical security. To facilitate its hacking and surveillance goals, the NSA puts backdoors into popular hardware and software products, which Schneier accuses the NSA of doing. However, this practice leaves users unprotected from other bad actors.

Last but not least, Schneier calls for a fundamental shift in data and the internet in the third section, "What to Do About It," starting with the following general principles:
- Pursue security and privacy.
- Prioritize security over surveillance.
- Ensure transparency across government and private sectors.
- Strengthen oversight and accountability.

He offers many solutions to government surveillance, including improving oversight of the IC and the NSA by Congress and the Privacy and Civil Liberties Oversight Board, enhancing whistleblower protection, reverting to targeted surveillance with judicial approval for a warrant, and dispersing the NSA into smaller entities. Schneier suggests corporations hold private companies (such as Crowdstrike[119]) liable for privacy violations, regulate data collection and use, give people inviolable rights to their data, and fight government surveillance in court. The book ends with an optimistic message about what individuals can do to mitigate harm - from noticing surveillance and discussing it with others to altering personal privacy settings.

The misuse of surveillance technology poses a grave threat to civil liberties, human rights, and democratic principles. It calls for a collective effort to establish transparent and accountable frameworks that safeguard individual privacy, ensure proper oversight, and prevent authoritarian practices. Only through such measures can we mitigate the risks associated with the unchecked proliferation of surveillance technologies and protect the foundations of free and democratic societies.

The work of independent journalists and whistleblowers, such as the collaborative efforts of Forbidden Stories and their "Pegasus Project," has been instrumental in exposing the global reach and misuse of Pegasus. Through their investigative reporting, they have brought to light

---

[119] https://www.crowdstrike.com/platform/

the scale of abuse facilitated by this surveillance tool, revealing the targeted surveillance of journalists, activists, and political figures in various countries. The revelations surrounding the misuse of Pegasus and the extensive research conducted by organizations, journalists, and academics demonstrate the urgent need for comprehensive reforms in surveillance practices. There is a pressing need for robust legislation and oversight mechanisms to prevent the abuse of surveillance technologies and protect fundamental rights and freedoms.

Investigations conducted by numerous organizations and researchers, including Citizen Lab and Amnesty International, have shed light on the extent of abuse facilitated by this powerful surveillance tool. Citizen Lab, a renowned interdisciplinary research group based at the University of Toronto, has been at the forefront of uncovering the misuse of Pegasus spyware. Their investigations have revealed how governments have deployed this highly invasive software to target human rights defenders, activists, and journalists worldwide. Through sophisticated techniques, Pegasus enables the surveillance and monitoring of individuals' phones, granting unauthorized access to their private communications, including messages, emails, and calls.

In their report titled "Hide and Seek: Tracking NSO Group's Pegasus Spyware"[120], Citizen Lab documented multiple cases of Pegasus being deployed against individuals targeted for their activism or critical voices. The report details instances where activists, lawyers, journalists, and government officials were subjected to surveillance and harassment using Pegasus. The revelations demonstrate the gravity of the threat posed by this surveillance technology, as it empowers authorities to intrude upon private lives, curtail freedoms, and violate fundamental human rights.

Likewise, Amnesty International investigations have provided compelling evidence of governments leveraging this spyware to suppress dissent and silence voices critical of their policies. By targeting journalists, activists, and human rights defenders, Pegasus has been used to undermine freedom of expression, intimidate individuals, and impede the work of those advocating for social justice and political reform. Claudio Guarnieri[121], a senior technologist at Amnesty International's Security Lab, has extensively analyzed the technical aspects of Pegasus and its deployment. His expertise has been instrumental in uncovering the operation and capabilities of this surveillance software.

---

[120] https://cyberir.mit.edu/?q=hide-and-seek-tracking-nso-group%E2%80%99s-pegasus-spyware-operations-45-countries

[121] https://www.forbes.com/profile/claudio-guarnieri/

The case of Pegasus serves as a wake-up call, exposing the potential for surveillance technology to be weaponized against those who challenge authority and advocate for human rights. Establishing clear guidelines and regulations to govern such technologies is essential, ensuring they are employed solely for legitimate purposes, such as national security and preventing serious crimes. In response to the Pegasus revelations and similar cases, calls for global action have been made to address the abuse of surveillance technology. Human rights organizations, academic institutions, and activists have emphasized international cooperation's importance in developing comprehensive legal frameworks and establishing accountability mechanisms. Efforts are underway to strengthen existing human rights conventions and treaties to encompass the challenges posed by modern surveillance practices. Corporations' collection and analysis of personal data without proper consent or transparency raise risks to individuals' privacy and personal autonomy.

The potential for abuse and misuse of surveillance technology presents severe threats to civil liberties, human rights, and democratic governance. Authors and academics such as Shoshana Zuboff, Naomi Klein, and Rebecca MacKinnon, among others, have extensively examined these risks. The targeted surveillance of political dissidents, activists, and journalists and the corporate exploitation of personal data underscore the urgent need for robust legal frameworks, transparency, and accountability in surveillance technology. Protecting fundamental principles of fairness, justice, and democratic governance requires vigilance in addressing the potential for abuse and misuse in surveillance.

Mass surveillance carries unintended consequences that transcend its intended purposes. The erosion of social trust, the impact on free speech and dissent, and the potential for abuse and misuse of surveillance technology raise significant concerns. These consequences undermine democratic values, hinder free expression, and threaten individual liberties and societal stability. It is essential to foster awareness, promote transparency, and establish robust legal and ethical frameworks to ensure the responsible and accountable use of surveillance technologies.

Chapter 6
Government Surveillance and National Security

"Those who would give up essential Liberty, to purchase a little temporary Safety, deserve neither Liberty nor Safety."

Benjamin Franklin

Government surveillance plays a pivotal role in national security efforts, particularly in the context of the "war against terror." Our objective in this chapter is to dispassionately consider the multifaceted aspects of government surveillance in the name of national security, exploring its role, legality, morality, and impact on international relations.

Post-9/11 we witnessed a significant shift in national security strategies, with governments around the world increasingly relying on surveillance as a central component of their counterterrorism measures. The aim is to gather intelligence, identify potential threats, and prevent terrorist activities. Surveillance technologies, both overt and covert, have been employed to monitor communications, track movements, and collect data on individuals suspected of involvement in terrorism or other criminal activities. To understand the legal and moral dimensions of government surveillance in the name of national security, it is essential to examine the tension between security and civil liberties. Governments argue that surveillance measures are necessary to safeguard citizens and maintain public safety.One of the key justifications for mass surveillance employed by governments is the utilization of legislation that grants expanded surveillance powers, such as the USA PATRIOT Act[122] in the United States. Enacted in the aftermath of the 9/11 terrorist attacks, the USA PATRIOT Act significantly expanded the authority of law enforcement and intelligence agencies to conduct surveillance activities in the name of national security. Proponents of the USA PATRIOT Act argue that it provides the necessary tools to detect and prevent terrorist activities by enhancing information sharing between intelligence agencies, facilitating surveillance of suspected individuals, and allowing for the collection of a wide range of data, including phone records, financial transactions, and internet communications. They contend that the Act strikes a balance between national security imperatives and individual privacy rights by including certain safeguards and oversight mechanisms.

---

[122] https://en.wikipedia.org/wiki/Patriot_Act

Supporters of the legislation assert that the evolving nature of modern threats necessitates an adaptive and proactive approach to intelligence gathering. They argue that the USA PATRIOT Act enables law enforcement and intelligence agencies to stay ahead of potential threats by leveraging advanced surveillance technologies and data analysis techniques. According to them, the Act provides the necessary legal framework to identify and disrupt terrorist networks, prevent attacks, and safeguard national security interests.

However, critics of the USA PATRIOT Act raise concerns about its potential for abuse and its impact on civil liberties. They argue that the Act grants broad surveillance powers with insufficient oversight and accountability measures. Critics point out that the Act allows for the collection of large amounts of data without requiring individualized suspicion or warrants, leading to the potential for dragnet surveillance and the monitoring of innocent individuals.

Prominent legal scholars and civil liberties advocates, such as David Cole, professor of law at Georgetown University Law Center[123], have criticized the USA PATRIOT Act for infringing upon privacy rights and undermining democratic principles. In his book "Enemy Aliens: Double Standards and Constitutional Freedoms in the War on Terrorism," Cole argues that the Act's provisions give the government sweeping surveillance powers, including access to personal information and the ability to conduct secret searches, without sufficient checks and balances.

Moreover, The revelations brought forth by whistleblowers have played a significant role in exposing the extent of mass surveillance practices and the potential abuses associated with them. The impact of whistleblowers like Edward Snowden and others have been profound. They have shed light on the hidden aspects of mass surveillance justified under legislation like the USA PATRIOT Act. These revelations have sparked debates on privacy, civil liberties, and government accountability, prompting a reevaluation of surveillance practices and the need for greater transparency.

As discussed previously one of the most prominent whistleblowers is Edward Snowden, a former contractor for the National Security Agency (NSA) in the United States. However there have been many more whistleblowers who perhaps not releasing the volume of confidential files that Snowden did nevertheless contributed greatly to a more resolved understanding of the extent of this surveillance. These include Chelsea Manning[124], formerly known as Bradley Manning, leaked classified documents to WikiLeaks, including the infamous "Collateral Murder"

[123] https://en.wikipedia.org/wiki/David_D._Cole

[124] https://en.wikipedia.org/wiki/Chelsea_Manning

video. The video depicted a U.S. military helicopter attack in Iraq, which resulted in the deaths of Iraqi civilians and journalists[125]. Manning's leaks also included diplomatic cables that exposed government misconduct and human rights abuses[126]. While Manning's disclosures were not primarily focused on surveillance, they highlighted the need for transparency and accountability in government actions. Likewise, William Binney[127], a former intelligence official at the NSA, became a whistleblower by disclosing the agency's data collection programs. He revealed the existence of Stellar Wind, a surveillance program[128] that involved the bulk collection of Americans' communications data without proper legal authorization. Binney's revelations highlighted the widespread collection of domestic communications data and raised concerns about the potential for abuse and violations of privacy rights. Thomas Drake, a former senior executive at the NSA, exposed wasteful and ineffective surveillance programs[129]. He raised concerns about the agency's Trailblazer project, which aimed to develop advanced data analysis capabilities but suffered from cost overruns and technical failures. Drake's disclosures revealed the mismanagement and questionable practices within the intelligence community, underscoring the need for accountability and oversight. And lastly Mark Klein, a former technician at AT&T, revealed the existence of Room 641A[130], a secret surveillance facility operated by the NSA. This facility intercepted and analyzed vast amounts of internet and telephone communications passing through AT&T's infrastructure[131]. Klein's disclosures highlighted the collaboration between telecommunications companies and intelligence agencies in conducting mass surveillance activities.

These whistleblowers, along with others like Jesselyn Radack[132], Thomas Tamm[133], and John Kiriakou[134], have collectively exposed the potential abuses of mass surveillance practices justified under legislation like the USA PATRIOT Act. Their actions have prompted public debates,

---

[125] https://www.youtube.com/watch?v=UaqY12VHFv4

[126] https://www.theguardian.com/world/2013/aug/05/bradley-manning-leak-foreign-policy-sentencing

[127] https://www.pbs.org/wgbh/pages/frontline/government-elections-politics/united-states-of-secrets/the-frontline-interview-william-binney/

[128] https://en.wikipedia.org/wiki/Stellar_Wind

[129] https://www.newyorker.com/magazine/2011/05/23/the-secret-sharer

[130] https://en.wikipedia.org/wiki/Room_641A

[131] https://www.youtube.com/watch?v=KqeMkv5FHfU

[132] https://en.wikipedia.org/wiki/Jesselyn_Radack

[133] https://en.wikipedia.org/wiki/Thomas_Tamm

[134] https://www.newyorker.com/magazine/2013/04/01/the-spy-who-said-too-much

legal challenges, and policy reforms aimed at striking a balance between national security and individual privacy rights.. In response to concerns over privacy and civil liberties, efforts have been made to reform and enhance oversight of surveillance practices. For example, The USA FREEDOM Act[135], enacted in 2015, represents an important legislative response to the concerns raised regarding the potential abuses associated with mass surveillance justified under the USA PATRIOT Act. Arguably, the provisions and implications of the USA FREEDOM Act were intended to to curtail excesses, impose limitations on bulk data collection, and enhance transparency and accountability within the realm of government surveillance.

One key aspect of the USA FREEDOM Act is its aim to curtail bulk data collection practices[136]. The act introduced reforms to restrict the National Security Agency's (NSA) ability to collect and store bulk telephony metadata. Instead, the act mandated that telecommunications companies retain the data, which could then be accessed by intelligence agencies through a targeted approach with court approval. This shift was intended to strike a balance between national security interests and individual privacy rights. The USA FREEDOM Act introduced stricter limitations on government surveillance. It established a more rigorous legal framework for obtaining data through the Foreign Intelligence Surveillance Court (FISC)[137] by requiring a "specific selection term" for the targeted collection of records. This provision aimed to prevent the indiscriminate collection of data and ensure that surveillance requests were more narrowly tailored to individuals of interest.

Transparency and accountability measures were crucial components of the USA FREEDOM Act. The act required the declassification of significant FISC decisions to provide greater insight into the legal interpretations guiding surveillance activities. Additionally, it established a panel of experts, known as the Privacy and Civil Liberties Oversight Board (PCLOB), to provide independent oversight and review of government surveillance programs[138]. The PCLOB plays a vital role in evaluating the legality, efficacy, and impact of surveillance activities on civil liberties.

While the USA FREEDOM Act represented a significant step towards addressing surveillance concerns, it received mixed reactions from various stakeholders. Some argued that the reforms did not go far enough and that additional safeguards were necessary to protect privacy rights.

---

[135] https://en.wikipedia.org/wiki/USA_Freedom_Act

[136] https://iapp.org/news/a/the-usa-freedom-act-explained

[137] https://www.fisc.uscourts.gov/

[138] https://www.brennancenter.org/our-work/analysis-opinion/privacy-and-civil-liberties-oversight-board-embraces-surveillance-reforms

Critics contended that the act still allowed for significant surveillance powers and did not fully address the issue of mass data collection. However, proponents of the act emphasized that it marked an important shift towards greater transparency, accountability, and judicial oversight.

Several authors and academics have analyzed and provided insights into the USA FREEDOM Act and its implications[139]. Jennifer Granick, in her book "American Spies: Modern Surveillance, Why You Should Care, and What to Do About It"[140], discusses the USA FREEDOM Act as an attempt to rein in surveillance powers and improve accountability. She explores the challenges of balancing security and civil liberties. Similarly, David Cole, in his book "Enemy Aliens: Double Standards and Constitutional Freedoms in the War on Terrorism," offers an analysis of the act's impact on civil liberties and government surveillance practices. The USA FREEDOM Act represents a significant milestone in the ongoing debate surrounding government surveillance and its impact on civil liberties. By curbing excesses, imposing stricter limitations on bulk data collection, and enhancing transparency and accountability measures, the act sought to address concerns raised under the USA PATRIOT Act. While the act received both praise and criticism, it symbolizes a commitment to striking a balance between national security interests and the protection of individual privacy rights. The ongoing examination and refinement of surveillance laws and practices remain essential to ensure that governmental surveillance activities align with democratic values and respect fundamental rights

The use of legislation such as the USA PATRIOT Act to justify mass surveillance underscores the ongoing debate surrounding the balance between national security and civil liberties. While proponents argue that such measures are essential for countering terrorist threats, critics emphasize the need for robust oversight, accountability, and respect for privacy rights. The tension between security imperatives and individual freedoms requires ongoing scrutiny and careful consideration to ensure that surveillance activities are conducted within the boundaries of the law while safeguarding civil liberties.

David Cole, the previously mentioned academic and professor of law at Georgetown University, has also made significant contributions to the analysis of the legal and ethical aspects of government surveillance. In his influential book, "Enemy Aliens: Double Standards and Constitutional Freedoms in the War on Terrorism"[141], Cole dissects the complex relationship between national security and civil liberties in the context of government surveillance. Cole's

[139] https://www.youtube.com/watch?v=L_uXFmsUV98

[140] https://www.amazon.com/American-Spies-Modern-Surveillance-Should/dp/1107501857

[141] https://www.amazon.com/Enemy-Aliens-Standards-Constitutional-Terrorism/dp/1565849388

work critically examines the impact of government surveillance practices on constitutional protections and individual rights. He highlights the potential dangers posed by unchecked surveillance powers, emphasizing the need for robust oversight mechanisms to safeguard civil liberties. Through extensive research and analysis, Cole sheds light on the delicate balance that must be struck between security imperatives and the preservation of fundamental freedoms. In "Enemy Aliens," Cole explores how government surveillance, justified under the guise of national security, can lead to the erosion of civil liberties. He raises important questions about the scope of government authority, the potential for overreach, and the need for transparency and accountability in surveillance practices. Cole's book underscores the crucial role of the legal system in ensuring that surveillance activities are conducted within the bounds of the Constitution and that individual rights are protected.

Drawing on his expertise as a legal scholar, Cole highlights the need for robust legal frameworks and judicial oversight to prevent abuses of surveillance powers[142]. He argues for the establishment of effective checks and balances to strike an appropriate balance between security concerns and the protection of civil liberties. Cole's analysis challenges policymakers, legal professionals, and the public to critically examine the implications of government surveillance and to actively engage in shaping laws and policies that safeguard individual rights. Cole's work is widely recognized and respected in academic and legal circles. His insightful analysis contributes to the ongoing debate surrounding government surveillance and serves as a valuable resource for those interested in understanding the legal and ethical dimensions of national security practices. By raising crucial questions and advocating for meaningful oversight and accountability, Cole's scholarship provides an essential framework for evaluating the implications of government surveillance in contemporary society.

In addition to David Cole, other notable academics and authors have also explored the legal and ethical dimensions of government surveillance. Previously mentioned Jennifer Granick, also examines the legal framework surrounding government surveillance, highlighting the need for comprehensive reform to protect privacy rights. Furthermore. Scholars such as Laura K. Donohue, author of "The Future of Foreign Intelligence: Privacy and Surveillance in a Digital Age"[143] provides in-depth analyses of the legal and policy implications of government surveillance in the digital era. Donohue examines the tension between privacy and national security, emphasizing the importance of striking the right balance through legislative and judicial measures.

---

[142] https://www.youtube.com/watch?v=hVclObff6fc

[143] https://www.amazon.com/Future-Foreign-Intelligence-Surveillance-Inalienable/dp/0190235381

These scholars, among others, contribute to the academic discourse on government surveillance, enriching our understanding of the legal and ethical complexities involved. Their research and analysis provide a foundation for informed discussions and policymaking, ultimately shaping the future of government surveillance practices and their impact on civil liberties.

The impact of government surveillance extends beyond domestic borders and has profound implications for international relations. Revelations of extensive surveillance programs, such as those disclosed by Edward Snowden, have strained diplomatic relationships between countries. The global community became acutely aware of the extent to which governments were collecting and analyzing data on both their own citizens and foreign individuals. These revelations caused diplomatic tensions, with some countries expressing outrage over the violation of privacy and the erosion of trust.

A notable example that vividly illustrates the impact of government surveillance on international relations is the diplomatic fallout between the United States and its European allies following the revelations brought forth by Edward Snowden[144]. The disclosure of classified documents revealed that the U.S. National Security Agency (NSA) had been engaged in extensive surveillance activities, including the interception of communications involving European leaders[145].

The revelations sent shockwaves throughout Europe, triggering a significant diplomatic uproar and straining transatlantic relations. European countries, such as Germany, France, and Spain, expressed outrage and concern over the violation of their leaders' privacy and the breach of trust between longstanding allies. The scale and scope of the surveillance practices were deeply unsettling, leading to widespread protests and calls for accountability.

The Snowden disclosures prompted European nations to demand explanations from the United States and seek assurances regarding the respect for privacy and the protection of their citizens' rights[146]. The European Union summoned U.S. ambassadors and conducted investigations into the extent of the surveillance activities[147]. In a resolution, they called for the suspension of data-

---

[144] https://www.bbc.com/news/world-us-canada-24664045

[145] https://www.theguardian.com/world/interactive/2013/nov/01/snowden-nsa-files-surveillance-revelations-decoded#section/1

[146] https://www.bbc.com/news/world-us-canada-23123964

[147] https://maint.loc.gov/law/help/intelligence-activities/europeanunion.php

sharing agreements and emphasized the need to uphold privacy rights and data protection standards. The diplomatic fallout between the United States and its European allies had far-reaching consequences. It prompted a reassessment of intelligence-sharing agreements, with European countries seeking to enhance their own intelligence capabilities and reduce reliance on U.S. surveillance infrastructure. The revelations also fueled debates about the need for stronger safeguards, transparency, and accountability in surveillance practices, not only within individual countries but also in international cooperation and intelligence-sharing frameworks.

The Snowden disclosures had implications beyond the transatlantic relationship. They led to a broader reevaluation of global surveillance practices and their impact on international relations. Countries worldwide, including Brazil, India, and Indonesia, expressed concerns about the reach and implications of mass surveillance[148]. The revelations sparked discussions within international organizations, such as the United Nations, on the need for stronger protections of privacy and human rights.

Academics and researchers have extensively examined the repercussions of the Snowden disclosures on international relations. Richard J. Aldrich, a professor of international security at the University of Warwick, explores the impact of the disclosures on intelligence sharing and cooperation among allies in his book "GCHQ: The Uncensored Story of Britain's Most Secret Intelligence Agency"[149], Aldrich provides insights into how the revelations strained relationships between intelligence agencies and affected global security dynamics. The case study of the Snowden disclosures serves as a powerful reminder of how government surveillance can have far-reaching consequences beyond domestic borders. It highlights the delicate balance between security imperatives and the respect for privacy and civil liberties in the international arena. The fallout between the United States and its European allies underscores the need for greater transparency, accountability, and respect for privacy rights in intelligence activities to preserve trust and uphold fundamental democratic values in the global community.

Ron Deibert[150], the director of the Citizen Lab at the Munk School of Global Affairs at the University of Toronto, is another highly influential scholar who has made significant contributions to the field of international relations and government surveillance. Deibert's expertise lies in the intersection of technology, human rights, and global security, making him a key figure in understanding the implications of government surveillance on international

---

[148] https://ecpr.eu/Events/Event/SectionDetails/850

[149] https://www.amazon.co.uk/GCHQ-Uncensored-Britains-Secret-Intelligence/dp/0007312660

[150] https://deibert.citizenlab.ca/bio/

relations. His book on the topic "Black Code: Surveillance, Privacy, and the Dark Side of the Internet"[151] provides a comprehensive analysis of the global implications of government surveillance. The book is an essay into the intricate ways in which surveillance technologies and practices have permeated societies worldwide, affecting not only individual privacy but also the dynamics of international relations. Deibert explores the far-reaching consequences of government surveillance, including its impact on diplomacy, human rights, and global security. He uncovers how governments exploit surveillance tools to gain an advantage in diplomatic negotiations, intelligence gathering, and geopolitical power struggles. By examining real-world case studies, Deibert sheds light on the intricate relationship between government surveillance and international relations. One such case study explored by Deibert is the targeting of dissidents and activists through surveillance technology. He highlights how governments, including authoritarian regimes, utilize surveillance to suppress dissent and control populations[152]. Deibert's research emphasizes the detrimental effects of such practices on civil liberties, human rights, and the integrity of international relations. Deibert's work also underscores the need for robust governance mechanisms, transparency, and accountability in the realm of government surveillance. He advocates for the development of international norms and regulations to safeguard individual rights and prevent abuses of surveillance technologies.

The contributions of Ron Deibert extend beyond Black Code. As the director of the Citizen Lab, Deibert leads a team of researchers and technologists who investigate and expose cases of government surveillance and digital threats. The Citizen Lab's reports and findings have had a significant impact on public awareness and policy discussions surrounding government surveillance and its consequences for international relations[153]. In addition to Ron Deibert's work, other academics and researchers have also made significant contributions to the study of government surveillance and its impact on international relations. Richard A. Clarke[154], a former U.S. government official and cybersecurity expert, explores the intersection of national security and digital surveillance in his book "Cyber War: The Next Threat to National Security and What to Do About It"[155] Clarke provides insights into how government surveillance practices shape and influence international relations in the context of cybersecurity threats.

---

[151] https://www.amazon.com/Black-Code-Surveillance-Privacy-Internet/dp/0771025351

[152] https://www.researchgate.net/publication/377429545_Digital_Authoritarianism_as_a_Modern_Threat_to_Democratic_Stability_Restriction_of_Freedom_or_Network_Politicization

[153] https://citizenlab.ca/2023/11/bill-c26-analysis-and-recommendations/

[154] https://en.wikipedia.org/wiki/Richard_A._Clarke

[155] https://www.amazon.com/Cyber-War-Threat-National-Security/dp/0061962244

Government surveillance in the name of national security has become a prominent feature of contemporary security strategies. While governments argue that it is necessary for protecting citizens and maintaining public safety, concerns persist regarding the legality, morality, and impact on civil liberties. Scholars like David Cole and Ron Deibert have critically analyzed the legal and ethical dimensions of government surveillance, offering insights into the tension between security and individual rights. Additionally, the impact of government surveillance on international relations, exemplified by the Snowden disclosures, highlights the diplomatic ramifications and the erosion of trust between nations. As the discourse surrounding government surveillance continues, it is crucial to strike a balance that upholds security while safeguarding civil liberties and preserving international cooperation.

Chapter 7
The Global Surveillance Network

"The price of freedom is eternal vigilance."

- Thomas Jefferson

The advancement of technology and the interconnectedness of the modern world have facilitated the emergence of a global surveillance network. Our focus is the intricate web of surveillance activities conducted by the National Security Agency (NSA) and the collaborative intelligence-sharing agreement known as the Five Eyes alliance. It examines the implications of this network on privacy, security, and human rights. Furthermore, it explores the potential future developments in global surveillance and their impact on human rights and civil liberties.

The role of the NSA and the Five Eyes alliance in global surveillance:

The NSA's central role in global surveillance is exemplified by its extensive capabilities, infrastructure, and the vast scope of data collection and analysis it undertakes. Academic research and real-life examples shed light on the collaboration between the NSA and its partners within the Five Eyes alliance, providing insights into how these entities cooperate in practice.

One notable case study that exemplifies the collaboration between the NSA and its allies is the PRISM program[156]. Edward Snowden's disclosures in 2013 revealed that the NSA, in collaboration with the Five Eyes partners, had direct access to data from major technology companies such as Google, Microsoft, and Facebook[157]. This partnership allowed the agencies to collect and analyze a wide range of user information, including emails, videos, and logs. The shared access to such vast repositories of data exemplifies the depth of cooperation between the NSA and its alliance partners.

---

[156] https://en.wikipedia.org/wiki/PRISM

[157] https://en.wikipedia.org/wiki/2010s_global_surveillance_disclosures

Furthermore, the intelligence-sharing practices within the Five Eyes alliance extend beyond accessing existing data. The agencies actively collaborate in intelligence operations and investigations. For instance, the joint surveillance of undersea fibre optic cables is a prominent area of cooperation. By tapping into these critical communication conduits, the NSA and its partners can intercept and monitor global telecommunications, gaining valuable insights into potential threats and intelligence activities[158].

Another significant example of collaboration within the alliance is the joint development and sharing of surveillance technologies. Scholars and investigative journalists have reported on instances where the NSA, in cooperation with its allies, has developed advanced tools for data collection and analysis. One example is the development of XKeyscore, a powerful data analysis tool that enables intelligence agencies to search and analyze vast amounts of intercepted data[159]. Through collaboration, the Five Eyes partners pool their expertise and resources to develop cutting-edge surveillance technologies, amplifying their surveillance capabilities on a global scale.

Moreover, intelligence sharing within the Five Eyes alliance has real-world implications for law enforcement and counterterrorism efforts. In high-profile cases, such as combating international terrorism, the alliance members exchange critical intelligence and coordinate joint operations[160]. These efforts involve sharing actionable information on individuals of interest, monitoring their activities, and ensuring the swift dissemination of intelligence across borders. The cooperative nature of the alliance enhances the effectiveness of counterterrorism efforts and strengthens national security.

One significant consequence of this collaboration is the potential erosion of privacy rights and civil liberties. The wide-ranging surveillance capabilities and practices enabled by the partnership between the NSA and its allies raise concerns about the scope of intrusion into individuals' private lives. Critics argue that the lack of transparency and accountability surrounding these surveillance activities undermines democratic values and the protection of individual rights.

The collaboration between the NSA and its partners within the Five Eyes alliance extends beyond data access and encompasses intelligence sharing, joint development of surveillance technologies, and coordinated law enforcement efforts. Real-life examples such as the PRISM program, undersea cable surveillance, and joint counterterrorism operations illustrate the depth of cooperation within the alliance. However, the implications of this collaboration for privacy

[158] https://engelsbergideas.com/essays/undersea-cables-and-the-vulnerability-of-american-power/

[159] https://www.theguardian.com/world/2013/jul/31/nsa-top-secret-program-online-data

[160] https://www.elibrary.imf.org/display/book/9798400204654/CH006.xml

rights and civil liberties necessitate ongoing scrutiny and a robust framework for transparency and accountability. By examining the works of researchers, whistleblowers like Edward Snowden, and investigative journalists, we can better understand the intricate dynamics and real-life consequences of the NSA and the Five Eyes alliance's cooperation in the global surveillance landscape.

The National Security Agency (NSA) occupies a central role in the global surveillance landscape due to its extensive capabilities, infrastructure, and the scale of data collection and analysis it conducts[161]. The collaboration between the NSA and its partners within the Five Eyes alliance (comprising the United States, the United Kingdom, Canada, Australia, and New Zealand) involves various methods of cooperation that offer insights into their collective impact on global surveillance.

One compelling aspect of their collaboration is the intelligence-sharing practices among the alliance members. This entails the exchange of classified information, including signals intelligence (SIGINT[162]), which enables the agencies to gain valuable insights into potential threats and intelligence activities. The sharing of actionable intelligence supports joint counterterrorism efforts, enabling swift responses and coordinated operations across borders.

Additionally, the Five Eyes alliance is known to engage in joint surveillance operations targeting various communication channels. For instance, they have been reported to collaborate in the monitoring of undersea fibre optic cables, which are crucial conduits for global telecommunications. By intercepting and analyzing the data transmitted through these cables, the alliance enhances its surveillance capabilities and gathers valuable intelligence.

The partnership between the NSA and its allies also extends to the development and sharing of surveillance technologies. Through joint research and development initiatives, the alliance members pool their expertise, resources, and technological advancements to create sophisticated tools for data collection, analysis, and decryption. These tools significantly enhance their surveillance capabilities and expand their ability to monitor and intercept communications across multiple platforms and services.

Furthermore, the Five Eyes alliance engages in shared access to data held by major technology companies. This cooperation involves direct access to information stored by companies such as Google, Microsoft, and Facebook, enabling the agencies to collect and analyze vast amounts of

[161] https://en.wikipedia.org/wiki/National_Security_Agency

[162] https://www.nsa.gov/Signals-Intelligence/Overview/

user data[163]. This access to data repositories contributes to the comprehensive surveillance efforts conducted by the alliance.

While the cooperation within the Five Eyes alliance strengthens national security efforts, it raises concerns about the potential erosion of privacy rights and civil liberties. The extensive surveillance capabilities and practices facilitated by this collaboration have prompted debates about the balance between security and individual freedoms. Critics argue that the lack of transparency, accountability, and oversight surrounding these surveillance activities undermines democratic values and poses risks to privacy.

The cooperation between the NSA and its partners within the Five Eyes alliance involves intelligence sharing, joint surveillance operations, collaborative technology development, and shared access to data held by major technology companies. These cooperative efforts enhance the capabilities of the alliance in gathering intelligence, conducting counterterrorism operations, and monitoring global communications. However, the impact on privacy and civil liberties necessitates ongoing scrutiny and the establishment of robust mechanisms for transparency, accountability, and the protection of individual rights. By examining the works of researchers and academics, we can gain a deeper understanding of the specific methods and implications of the cooperation within the NSA and the Five Eyes alliance in the global surveillance network.

Moreover, independent news outlets such as The Guardian, The Intercept, and Der Spiegel have published numerous articles based on leaked documents and insider sources, offering comprehensive insights into the Five Eyes alliance's surveillance practices[164]. Through meticulous investigative reporting, these outlets have exposed programs like PRISM, which involves direct data access from major technology companies, and TEMPORA[165], which involves the interception and storage of vast amounts of global internet communications.

The investigative journalism community's efforts have brought to light the potential ramifications of the Five Eyes alliance's activities on privacy, civil liberties, and international relations. By scrutinizing and exposing these practices, investigative journalists have contributed to public discourse, prompting debates on the balance between security and individual rights.

---

[163] https://www.nsa.gov/About/Cybersecurity-Collaboration-Center/

[164] https://www.lawfaremedia.org/article/newly-disclosed-documents-five-eyes-alliance-and-what-they-tell-us-about-intelligence-sharing

[165] https://www.amnesty.org.uk/why-taking-government-court-mass-spying-gchq-nsa-tempora-prism-edward-snowden

It is worth noting that the disclosures made by investigative journalists have often faced pushback from government entities, which emphasize the necessity of surveillance for national security purposes[166]. However, the crucial role of investigative journalism in holding power accountable and informing the public about the inner workings of the Five Eyes alliance cannot be overstated.

investigative journalists have played a vital role in uncovering the practices and implications of the Five Eyes alliance. Their reporting has provided valuable insights into the surveillance activities of the alliance, exposing programs and methods employed to gather intelligence and monitor global communications. By highlighting the potential impact on privacy and civil liberties, investigative journalists have stimulated public discussions and raised important questions about the balance between security and individual rights in the context of global surveillance.

The impact of the global surveillance network on privacy and security

This section delves into the multifaceted impact of the global surveillance network on privacy and security. It examines the challenges posed by the vast collection of personal data, the potential for abuses, and the erosion of privacy rights. Drawing on scholarly work by authors such as Glenn Greenwald, Edward Snowden, and Kate Crawford, and in analyzing real-world examples and case studies that illustrate the consequences of this network on individual privacy. It also explores the implications for security, questioning the effectiveness of mass surveillance in preventing and mitigating threats while emphasizing the potential risks associated with the accumulation of data in the hands of powerful entities.

The future of global surveillance and its potential impact on human rights

This section ventures into the future of global surveillance and its potential implications for human rights and civil liberties. We will explore the evolving landscape of surveillance technologies, including the rise of private surveillance companies and the increasing involvement of non-state actors. By referencing the works of experts such as Shoshana Zuboff, Yuval Noah Harari, and Evgeny Morozov, we will provide insights into the potential ramifications of these developments. It explores the ethical considerations and challenges arising from the expansion of surveillance capabilities, including the implications for freedom of expression, autonomy, and the right to privacy.

---

[166] https://cpijournalism.org/investigative-journalism-legal-ethical/

The fact that a comprehensive global surveillance network exists is not debated. It highlights the role of the NSA and the Five Eyes alliance in facilitating extensive data collection and analysis. We will critically examine the impact of this network on privacy, security, and human rights. By drawing upon the work of prominent scholars, researchers, and whistleblowers, it sheds light on the challenges posed by the lack of transparency, accountability, and potential for abuses. It is important now that we have explored some of the landscape of privacy issues to contemplate the implications of global surveillance on fundamental rights and freedoms, and on you as an individual.

Chapter 8

Protecting Your Privacy: Tips and Strategies for Protecting Your Privacy and Cultivating Privacy Awareness

"Privacy is not something that I'm merely entitled to, it's an absolute prerequisite."

Marlon Brando

As individuals become increasingly aware of the risks to their privacy in the ., it becomes crucial to equip them with practical strategies and foster privacy awareness. This chapter explores various proactive measures and practices that individuals can adopt to safeguard their personal information. It also emphasizes the significance of privacy awareness in making informed decisions that align with personal privacy preferences and values.

Section 1: Safeguarding personal information in the digital realm

Security and encryption: safeguarding digital communications

The security of confidential information and safeguarding sensitive data has become an increasing concern. Encryption is a powerful tool for safeguarding sensitive data and securing digital communication. We examine the critical role played by encryption. We will explore how to use it, and emphasize how it can help mitigate the risks of data interception and unauthorized access.

Increasingly, we are in a time of cyber threats and data breaches, and in this context, encryption is considered a formidable defense mechanism. Encryption involves encoding information using complex algorithms, rendering it unreadable to unauthorized individuals. In order to protect sensitive information from being intercepted and misused, encrypted messaging applications are commonly employed.

An overview of encryption

What is encryption, and how does it work? How do you determine which type of encryption is required? If you ask someone what kind of encryption they use, they may respond with specific encryption-based products, such as full-disk encryption, or a protocol, such as HTTPS. These products are designed to protect the data on a; however, these are the end products used to encrypt data. The underlying technology is the encryption algorithms that make these products and protocols work. These ensure that a third party cannot access the data without the correct key or password. Despite the difficulty many of us may have in comprehending mathematical ciphers, we can still utilize this fantastic process without advanced mathematical knowledge. You can benefit from it by understanding how and why encryption is used. And this makes it easier to comprehend its significance. Understanding how encryption works is our aim and this chapter which will provide an in-depth understanding by going over both the encryption process and the concept of cryptographic keys.

Cryptographic keys are used to generate the ciphertext. This text is unreadable in its ciphertext. It was created when perfectly readable material was scrambled by the mathematical algorithm. The algorithm converts information into ciphertext, i.e., the equivalent of the coded messages you played around with as a child, only much more complex. The ciphertext can be decrypted or reversed using the same encryption algorithm and key as the encryption process. The intended recipient reverses it.

Cryptographic keys are generated and stored securely during the initial encryption process to scramble the message. The keys are usually long strings of random characters that, although random, are unique in that these strings of characters are needed to reverse the encryption process conducted by the algorithm. Usually, only a limited number of random character strings (or keys) will perform this task. The ciphertext is decrypted with the knowledge of the key. An example of a symmetric encryption algorithm is AES, which uses only one key for encryption and decryption and is widely used, ranging from protecting computer data to securing credit card transactions. It is also used to encrypt sensitive information such as credit card numbers by primary online services and financial institutions, and the US government is also using it to secure sensitive data. AES stands for Advanced Encryption Standard[167]. It is a symmetric encryption algorithm (described further below). However, other commonly used symmetric encryption algorithms are usually defined by the length of the key in bits of information. One such example is the DES (Data Encryption Standard)[168], it is the older symmetric encryption algorithm that AES, and it uses a 56-bit key. While it was widely used in the past, its key size is considered too small by today's standards, making it vulnerable to brute-force attacks.

---

[167] https://www.geeksforgeeks.org/advanced-encryption-standard-aes/

[168] https://www.geeksforgeeks.org/difference-between-aes-and-des-ciphers/

Therefore, it is not recommended for new applications. Others include 3DES (Triple Data Encryption Standard), Blowfish, Twofish and Serpent. 3DES is an enhanced version of DES that applies DES three times with different keys. It uses a key length of 168 bits, providing a higher security level than DES. However, due to its slow speed and the availability of more efficient algorithms, 3DES is being phased out in favor of AES. Blowfish is a symmetric encryption algorithm designed to replace DES. It supports key sizes ranging from 32 bits to 448 bits, making it highly flexible. Blowfish is known for its fast encryption and decryption speed, and it has been widely used in various applications. Twofish supports key sizes up to 256 bits and is considered highly secure. Serpent is another symmetric encryption algorithm that supports key sizes up to 256 bits and is known for its strong security.

These symmetric encryption algorithms protect sensitive information during storage or transmission. They are applied in various scenarios, such as secure communication over networks, data encryption on storage devices, secure messaging protocols, virtual private networks (VPNs), and many other security-sensitive applications.

Outside of the basic idea of encryption algorithms and keys are three core concepts to understand. These are the generic names for classes of mathematical ciphers: Symmetric, Asymmetric, and Hashing[169].

Keeping data secret is the purpose of symmetric ciphers. A symmetric cipher is used to store and share secret information so that it can be read later on. We must be able to decrypt the data with a key to read it. Symmetric means that the same key is used to encrypt and decrypt the data, thus "symmetric". Imagine it as a lockbox. I have a secret message for you, so I put it in a box and locked it with a key. I then hand you the box so that you can open it. But you must also have a key. This is one of the significant challenges of symmetric ciphers. How can you create a lock box and its key and then distribute it to others without someone stealing or coping the key? We will come back to this problem shortly.

A symmetric key is extremely strong and capable of encrypting almost any message with the least effort, which is why symmetric ciphers are widely used to encrypt information such as hard drives, files, and emails[170]. Furthermore, it can encrypt data wirelessly and over the Internet. Asymmetric ciphers however are different and understanding them will help us solve the above key distribution problem. If symmetric encryption uses the same key for locking and unlocking,

[169] https://www.ibm.com/think/topics/cryptography-types

[170] https://www.cryptomathic.com/news-events/blog/symmetric-key-encryption-why-where-and-how-its-used-in-banking

it should be evident that asymmetric encryption uses a different key to unlock the device. Keeping the private keys private is essential while sharing the public keys is free. We call this pair of keys private/public key pairs. As we have discussed, asymmetric ciphers can encrypt only small amounts of data, so we can't use them to encrypt actual secret messages. Our application of asymmetric ciphers usually is limited to two primary purposes. The first is required distribution. I have a secret message encrypted with a symmetric cipher that I need to share with you, but you need the key. Once I receive your public key, I can lock the symmetric key (aka session key) so that only your private key can unlock it. In this scenario, although the public key is accessible to everyone worldwide, it is only capable of locking, not unlocking. The session key would then allow you to unlock the secret message. Until now, all of these factors support the concept of confidentiality as a security measure. We can also use this private/public key pair to digitally sign my message and confirm that it is me sending you this information. Since you have a copy of my public key, I can send you some data attached to my message and then encrypt it with my private key. Because my private key was used to lock it, only my public key can unlock it. Now, this little packet of data is not a secret—anyone can read it using my public key. The purpose was not to keep it a secret. Instead, it was to prove that I sent it. Since no one else has my private key, no one else could have sent this signed data packet. We call this process "authentication"[171].

Now the final type of algorithm is Hashing. Hashing differs from symmetric and asymmetric encryption in that we do not encrypt and then decrypt[172]. Hashing algorithms are irreversible. We must run our plaintext of any length to produce a digest through the hashing algorithm. The result is a fixed-length set of 0s and 1s. Although the original message can range from a single character to an entire set of encyclopedias, it does not matter how large or small the original message is. The digest will always be the same size. The digest that results will always be the same if I repeatedly put the same plaintext through the algorithm. Let us now return to the small data packet I signed with my digital signature. Where did this data come from? I can create a digest of my original message by running it through a hashing algorithm. Most digests range from 160 bits to 384 bits. My small packet of data is attached to this digest. Once you have completed the other encryption on my original plaintext, you can repeat the same hashing algorithm. If your version of the hash matches my version, you can rest assured that this is my original message and no one has tampered with it. In security terms, this is known as "message integrity".

[171] https://www.techtarget.com/searchsecurity/definition/authentication

[172] https://cybernews.com/security/hashing-vs-encryption/

You must understand the differences between symmetric and asymmetric encryption algorithms and their applications to use them effectively. An encrypting key is used in symmetric encryption to encrypt and decrypt the data simultaneously, whereas, in asymmetric encryption, the key is used separately for encrypting and decrypting the data. Aside from end-to-end encryption, another concept is essential to understand and that is non-reverse encryption. Non-reverse encryption ensures that the information transmitted will only be decrypted and accessible by the intended recipients. Only the communicating users who can read end-to-end encrypted messages can be viewed. There is a way to prevent possible eavesdroppers - such as internet providers or even the communication service provider - from accessing the cryptographic keys necessary to decrypt the conversation. The messages sent through popular messaging apps like WhatsApp or Signal are encrypted end-to-end so that only the sender and the receiver can view them. Using non-reverse encryption, it is impossible to decrypt or "unlock" encrypted messages without the specific key known only by the sender and recipient of the encrypted message. The encrypted message can only be decrypted or viewed if someone can access the key required to unlock it. If the message was intercepted, someone could not decrypt or view its contents.

The Importance of secure digital communications

With digital platforms playing a significant in communication, securing digital communications has never been more crucial. Encryption plays a vital role in ensuring the privacy and security of various digital communication methods, including messaging apps, email services, and voice calls[173].

In the world of secure messaging applications, end-to-end encryption stands out. Apps like Signal and WhatsApp employ end-to-end encryption, which means only the sender and the receiver can read each other's messages. This means that even if a hacker were to intercept the message, they wouldn't be able to read it. As such, end-to-end encryption is the best way to ensure secure communication between two parties. Email encryption services also play a significant role in safeguarding sensitive email data from unauthorized access. One notable example is Pretty Good Privacy (PGP)[174], which provides a mechanism for encrypting and decrypting email messages. By implementing email encryption services, individuals and organizations can protect the confidentiality of their email communications and prevent unauthorized parties from accessing their sensitive data.

---

[173] https://nandbox.com/the-role-of-end-to-end-encryption-in-securing-communication-on-messaging-platforms/

[174] https://en.wikipedia.org/wiki/Pretty_Good_Privacy

The protection of digital communications goes beyond individual privacy concerns. It extends to ensuring the security and integrity of sensitive information transmitted across digital platforms. By embracing encryption technologies and adhering to secure communication practices, individuals and organizations can mitigate the risks associated with data interception and unauthorized access. Encryption serves as a formidable defense mechanism against cyber threats and data breaches. Understanding the different types of encryption ciphers, such as symmetric, asymmetric, and hashing, allows individuals to make informed decisions regarding their use.

Being cautious about information shared online

Technology has seamlessly integrated into our daily lives. In this context, the notion of "mindful sharing" has gained paramount importance. As a principle, we need to conscientiously be aware and mindful of any information we share online[175]. By illuminating the potential repercussions of oversharing personal details, the perils of identity theft, and the necessity of configuring social media privacy settings, readers will be equipped with practical guidance to gauge the appropriateness of shared information and curtail their digital footprint.

The concept of mindful sharing entails the deliberate and cautious consideration of the potential impact before disseminating information online. For instance, individuals are advised to exercise caution when posting images or videos that may expose themselves or others to vulnerable situations, as the repercussions may prove unforeseen or undesirable. Mindful sharing fosters a judicious approach to the type and extent of personal information divulged online. By adopting these practices, individuals can fortify their privacy, shield themselves from malicious activities, and retain a semblance of control over their digital identities. Consequently, users are advised to exercise prudence when revealing sensitive details such as financial information, social security numbers, or residential addresses[176].

The ramifications of oversharing personal details can reverberate through both the virtual and tangible realms. Information shared online, even seemingly innocuous, can be harvested, consolidated, and potentially exploited by various entities including cybercriminals, data brokers, and individuals with malicious intent[177]. It is essential to comprehend that once information permeates the boundary from the physical to the digital world, retractions or erasure become arduous tasks, exposing individuals to potential harm to their reputation,

---

[175] https://mediasmarts.ca/digital-media-literacy/digital-issues/authenticating-information/ethics-sharing-information-online/think-you-share

[176] https://www.digitalguardian.com/blog/what-sensitive-information-how-classify-protect-it

[177] https://journalistsresource.org/media/fake-news-bad-information-online-research/

financial fraud, or even physical peril. For instance, malevolent actors can exploit this information to track an individual's movements or subject them to scams and phishing emails[178].

Among the gravest risks associated with indiscriminate sharing of personal information online is identity theft—an affliction that afflicts thousands of individuals annually, with many cases going unreported. As previously highlighted, cybercriminals can painstakingly construct an individual's identity to facilitate various fraudulent activities, including unauthorized financial transactions, opening fraudulent accounts, or assuming someone's identity entirely. However, exercising caution and minimizing the exposure of personal information can significantly diminish the likelihood of falling prey to identity theft and other online security threats. Implementing measures such as employing robust passwords, avoiding public Wi-Fi networks, and refraining from clicking suspicious links in emails serve as pillars of protection against online security risks.

Social media platforms form the bedrock of digital interactions and information sharing. Understanding and optimizing the privacy settings offered by these platforms constitutes a critical imperative. By configuring privacy settings, individuals can restrict the visibility of their posts, regulate access to their profiles and personal information, and exert control over the degree to which their data is disseminated to third-party applications. Regularly reviewing and updating privacy settings becomes instrumental in upholding authority over one's online presence. It is important to note that despite stringent privacy measures, users must remain cognizant of the potential for data to be shared and utilized by third-party applications and websites. Therefore, familiarizing oneself with platform terms and conditions ensures users remain comfortable with how their data is employed.

Five practical tips for mindful sharing

TIP 1 - Evaluate the Purpose: Prior to divulging information, ascertain the underlying purpose and consider whether it is necessary or appropriate. Weigh the potential implications against the anticipated benefits,

TIP 2 - Limit Personal Details: Exercise discretion in sharing sensitive personal information, such as complete addresses, phone numbers, social security numbers, or financial details, unless absolutely essential. Exercise caution when divulging location data and contemplate disabling geotagging features on devices,

---

[178] https://www.cyberdefensemagazine.com/how-bad-actors/

TIP 3 - Selective Sharing: Employ discretion when determining the audience for posts and information. Leverage social media privacy settings to tailor visibility, ensuring that only trusted individuals have access to the shared content. This strategic approach promotes a controlled flow of information and minimizes exposure to potential risks,

TIP 4 - Be Wary of Online Requests: Exercise caution when confronted with requests for personal information or financial transactions online. Verify the authenticity of websites, emails, or messages before divulging sensitive data. Maintaining a healthy skepticism and actively verifying the legitimacy of such requests can shield individuals from falling victim to scams or data breaches,

TIP 5 - Regularly Review Privacy Settings: Dedicate time to periodically review and update privacy settings across social media platforms and online services. Staying informed about the evolving policies and features of these platforms empowers users to make informed decisions about their personal information and the extent of its accessibility.

The responsibility of safeguarding personal information in the digital realm rests upon each individual. Mindful sharing serves as a guiding principle to navigate the dynamic landscape of online interactions. By thoughtfully considering the information shared, individuals can mitigate the risks associated with oversharing. Awareness of the consequences of divulging personal details, comprehension of the perils of identity theft, and active management of privacy settings on social media platforms all contribute to a secure online presence.

Implementing the practical tips for mindful sharing—evaluating the purpose of sharing, limiting personal details, practicing selective sharing, approaching online requests with caution, and regularly reviewing privacy settings—enables individuals to make informed decisions about the information they disclose and exercise greater control over their digital identities. By fostering a culture of prudence and responsibility, individuals can confidently engage with the digital world, preserving their privacy, and reaping the benefits of technology without compromising their security.

By heeding the call for prudence in the online sphere, individuals can navigate the complexities of digital interactions and protect their personal information. Through the deliberate assessment of shared information and the implementation of prudent measures, individuals assume greater control over their digital footprint, ensuring a safer and more secure digital presence

Bolstering security with robust passwords and two-factor authentication

Our lives are increasingly intertwined with online accounts and the significance of fortifying our defense cannot be overstated. Password security sounds like a dull topic, but it is critical in maintaining aspects of privacy. Strong and unique passwords for different sites and apps represent the "low handing fruit" of safeguarding our online presence. Furthermore, we willl introduce the concept of two-factor authentication (2FA) as an additional layer of protection and equips readers with step-by-step instructions on enabling 2FA across diverse online platforms and services. By embracing these practices, individuals can bolster their security and fortify their digital fortresses.

Passwords serve as the first line of defense in the realm of online security. Crafting robust passwords is not merely a matter of convenience; it is a necessity considering the growth of sophisticated cyber threats. Utilizing strong and unique passwords across various accounts fortifies our digital defenses, making it exponentially more challenging for malicious actors to gain unauthorized access.

Crafting a strong password demands careful consideration. Striking a balance between complexity and memorability is the key. Here are three critical tips to help.

TIP 1 - Length and Complexity: Opt for passwords that are at least 12 characters long, combining uppercase and lowercase letters, numbers, and special characters. Steer clear of common phrases or easily guessable patterns.

TIP 2 - Avoid Personal Information: Resist the temptation to use easily discoverable personal details, such as birthdays, pet names, or addresses, as elements of your password. Such information can be exploited through social engineering or data breaches.

TIP 3 - Uniqueness: Avoid reusing passwords across multiple accounts. Each account should have a distinct password to mitigate the impact of a potential breach. Consider using password managers to securely store and manage a multitude of unique passwords.

While strong passwords are a formidable defense, the addition of two-factor authentication (2FA) adds an extra layer of protection. 2FA verifies users' identities through two independent factors: something they know (such as a password) and something they possess (such as a mobile device).

Enabling 2FA is a prudent measure that significantly strengthens online security. The process varies across platforms and services, but the following six TIPS will help you.

TIP 1 - Select the Appropriate Method: Determine the 2FA method that best suits your needs. Common options include SMS verification codes, authentication apps (such as Google Authenticator or Authy), or hardware tokens.

TIP 2 - Enable 2FA on Online Platforms: Access the security or account settings of the platform or service you wish to secure. Look for the 2FA or multi-factor authentication (MFA) options and follow the provided instructions.

TIP 3 - Link Your Mobile Device: If opting for SMS verification codes, associate your mobile phone number with your account. You will receive a text message containing a unique code whenever you attempt to log in.

TIP 4 - Authentication Apps: If utilizing authentication apps, download and install the chosen app on your mobile device. Follow the app's instructions to link it to your account and generate one-time verification codes.

TIP 5 - Backup Codes: Many platforms provide backup codes that serve as a contingency in case you lose access to your primary 2FA method. Safeguard these codes in a secure location.

TIP 6 - Test the Setup: Once 2FA is enabled, perform a test login to ensure the authentication process functions smoothly. Familiarize yourself with the steps required to authenticate successfully.

Escalating cyber threats require the broad adoption of robust password practices. Augmenting this with two-factor authentication (2FA) is also emerging as an imperative to safeguard our digital lives. By creating strong and unique passwords, we fortify our first line of defense, making it arduous for cybercriminals to breach our accounts. The judicious use of 2FA adds an extra layer of protection, mitigating the risks of unauthorized access.

However, it is essential to acknowledge that password security and 2FA are not foolproof. As technology advances, so do the tactics employed by cybercriminals. Staying informed about emerging security measures and adapting to evolving threats is crucial in maintaining robust protection.

The landscape of password security is ever-evolving, with new challenges and advancements surfacing regularly. It is essential to stay informed and adapt our practices accordingly. Here are five key tips that should serve you well.

TIP 1 - Password Managers: As the number of online accounts we manage continues to grow, password managers offer a convenient solution. These tools generate and securely store complex passwords, alleviating the burden of memorization while ensuring uniqueness across accounts.

TIP 2 - Biometric Authentication: Biometric factors, such as fingerprints or facial recognition, are increasingly being integrated into authentication systems. These technologies offer a more convenient and secure means of accessing accounts, complementing traditional password-based security.

TIP 3 - Passwordless Authentication: The emergence of passwordless authentication methods seeks to eliminate passwords altogether. Techniques such as hardware tokens, cryptographic keys, or biometric factors provide alternative means of verifying identity, reducing the reliance on passwords.

TIP 4 - Multifactor Authentication: Going beyond 2FA, multifactor authentication (MFA) incorporates additional factors, such as biometrics or behavioral patterns, to further enhance security. MFA reinforces the barriers against unauthorized access, making it increasingly challenging for malicious actors to infiltrate accounts.

TIP 5 - Security Awareness: Education and awareness are vital components of maintaining strong password security. By promoting a culture of cybersecurity literacy, individuals become empowered to make informed decisions, recognize phishing attempts, and understand the importance of protecting their digital identities.

In an interconnected world where our personal and professional lives revolve around online platforms, ensuring the security of our accounts is of paramount importance. Employing strong and unique passwords serves as the foundation of our defense, bolstering our resilience against cyber threats. By embracing two-factor authentication (2FA) as an additional layer of security, we fortify our digital fortresses, making unauthorized access a formidable challenge.

Nevertheless, the realm of password security is dynamic, and cybercriminals continually seek new vulnerabilities to exploit. Staying vigilant and adapting to emerging security measures is crucial in our quest for robust protection. Whether through password managers, biometric authentication, or passwordless alternatives, embracing evolving technologies contributes to a safer digital world.

Ultimately, the responsibility for safeguarding our online accounts rests with each individual. By implementing strong password practices, embracing two-factor authentication, and remaining informed about emerging security measures, we fortify our defense and navigate the digital realm with confidence. Our digital fortresses stand strong, preserving our privacy, personal information, and digital identities in the face of evolving cyber threats.

Looking ahead, the collective efforts of individuals, technology providers, and regulatory bodies will shape the future of password security. Collaboration between these stakeholders is crucial to staying one step ahead of cybercriminals and maintaining the integrity of our online ecosystems.

Technology providers must continue to invest in research and development to enhance password security measures. This includes developing innovative authentication methods, improving encryption algorithms, and implementing advanced fraud detection systems. By prioritizing user security and privacy, technology companies can inspire trust and foster a safer digital environment.

Furthermore, regulatory bodies play a pivotal role in establishing standards and guidelines for password security practices. By promoting best practices, enforcing data protection regulations, and incentivizing organizations to prioritize user security, regulators can contribute to a more secure online landscape.

Individuals, on their part, must remain proactive in adopting and implementing strong password practices and embracing emerging security technologies. Regularly updating passwords, utilizing password managers, and enabling two-factor authentication should become ingrained habits in our digital lives. Additionally, staying informed about the latest cybersecurity threats and educating ourselves on phishing techniques and social engineering tactics empowers us to make informed decisions and protect our online accounts effectively.

The future of password security demands an ongoing commitment to continuous improvement. As technology evolves, so too must our security measures. Many journals warm of the need to continue to monitor and report on the advancements in password security, offering insights and analysis to help individuals navigate the ever-changing landscape of online security. The Harvard Business review and the Economist are examples of the commitment made in this regard[179]. Such a commitment is useful as increasingly the public requires trusted sources to help navigate the appropriate practice response to a new cyber threat.

Robust password security and the adoption of two-factor authentication are paramount in protecting our online accounts from unauthorized access. By employing strong and unique passwords, embracing emerging technologies, and fostering a security-conscious mindset, individuals can fortify their digital defense. The collaborative efforts of technology providers, regulatory bodies, and individuals will shape the future of password security, ensuring a safer and more secure digital world for all.

---

[179] https://hbr.org/2023/05/the-digital-world-is-changing-rapidly-your-cybersecurity-needs-to-keep-up

Regularly updating software

Keeping software up to date is essential in maintaining a secure digital environment. This section emphasizes the significance of software updates and patches in addressing vulnerabilities and protecting against cyber threats. It provides practical advice on enabling automatic updates and highlights the risks associated with using outdated software.

Harnessing the power of Virtual Private Networks (VPNs) for unparalleled online privacy

Today, where our digital footprints leave behind a trail of personal information, safeguarding our online privacy has become paramount. Enter Virtual Private Networks (VPNs), the vanguard of online privacy and security. There are a myriad of benefits in utilizing VPNs as a powerful shield against prying eyes. However, as has probably emerged already as a theme, these are not a panacea to ensure complete privacy protection. There are also a variety of options with VPNs - some better that others and some of no use at all. Selecting trustworthy VPN services is a thoughtful exercise and we explore the significance of comprehending VPN protocols, server locations, and logging policies, and that will empower readers to make informed choices when it comes to their selection and use of a VPN.

Virtual Private Networks (VPNs) stand as a formidable line of defense, elevating online privacy to unprecedented levels. By encrypting internet traffic and obfuscating users' IP addresses, VPNs offer a shield against eavesdropping, data surveillance, and intrusive tracking mechanisms. With VPNs, individuals can reclaim control over their digital presence, navigate the internet with anonymity, and protect their sensitive information from prying eyes.

The Benefits of VPNs are fourfold

BENEFIT 1 - Enhanced Privacy: VPNs create a secure tunnel between a user's device and the internet, encrypting all data transmitted. This ensures that sensitive information, such as login credentials, banking details, or personal communications, remains shielded from potential interceptions.

BENEFIT 2 - Geo-restriction Bypass: VPNs allow users to bypass geographical restrictions and access content that may be limited or censored in their region. By masking their IP address and routing internet traffic through servers located in different countries, individuals can enjoy unrestricted access to a global digital environments.

BENEFIT 3 - Public Wi-Fi Protection: Public Wi-Fi networks pose significant risks, as they are often vulnerable to malicious activities. VPNs provide an extra layer of security by encrypting data transmitted over these networks, safeguarding users from potential attacks and unauthorized access.

BENEFIT 4 - Anonymity and Identity Protection: By masking users' IP addresses, VPNs prevent websites, advertisers, and other entities from tracking online activities or building profiles based on browsing habits. This ensures a higher level of anonymity and protects users' digital identities.

However, not all VPNs are created equal. Selecting a reliable VPN requires careful consideration of several key factors. When choosing a VPN provider there are five key of issues to consider. These are

ISSUE 1 - VPN Protocols: The selection of an appropriate VPN protocol is crucial, as it determines the level of security and performance. Common protocols include OpenVPN, IKEv2/IPSec, and WireGuard. OpenVPN is widely regarded as secure and versatile, while IKEv2/IPSec offers fast and stable connections. WireGuard, a newer protocol, boasts simplicity and efficiency.

ISSUE 2 - Server Locations: The geographical distribution of VPN servers plays a vital role in unlocking geo-restricted content and optimizing connection speeds. A diverse range of server locations enables individuals to bypass geo-restrictions effectively and optimize connection speeds. A VPN provider with servers strategically placed in different regions offers greater flexibility and accessibility to global content.

ISSUE 3 - Logging Policies: Understanding a VPN provider's logging policies is imperative in preserving privacy. Ideally, opt for providers with strict no-logs policies, meaning they do not retain any identifiable user information. This ensures that even if compelled by legal authorities, the VPN provider cannot provide user data.

ISSUE 4 - Reputation and Trustworthiness: Thoroughly research VPN providers, taking into account their reputation, track record, and reviews from reputable sources. Trustworthy providers prioritize user privacy, transparency, and security, ensuring a reliable and dependable service.

ISSUE 5 - Performance and Reliability: Assess the performance and reliability of VPN services by considering factors such as connection speeds, server uptime, and customer support. A VPN that offers consistent and high-speed connections ensures a seamless and hassle-free online experience.

Virtual Private Networks (VPNs) have emerged as the bastions of online privacy and security. By encrypting internet traffic and masking users' IP addresses, VPNs empower individuals to reclaim control over their digital lives and safeguard their sensitive information from prying eyes. They provide enhanced privacy by creating secure tunnels that protect data transmission from potential interceptions. VPNs also enable individuals to bypass geo-restrictions, granting access to a global sources that would otherwise be off-limits. Moreover, VPNs offer crucial protection when using public Wi-Fi networks, shielding users from the inherent vulnerabilities of these environments. By obfuscating IP addresses, VPNs ensure anonymity and protect digital identities from tracking and profiling.

Section 2: Cultivating Privacy Awareness for Responsible Digital Citizenship

Understanding the Implications of Online Activities:

This section underscores the need for individuals to critically assess the implications of their online activities. It explores the potential consequences of sharing personal information, engaging with online platforms, and granting permissions to apps and services. It encourages individuals to consider the long-term impact of their actions and make informed decisions that align with their privacy preferences and values.

Safeguarding Privacy and Security through Digital Hygiene

Practicing good digital hygiene has become an indispensable necessity. Digital hygiene encompasses a set of habits and behaviors that prioritize privacy and security, safeguarding our online lives from potential threats. We will now consider some practical tips and guidance on cultivating a culture of digital hygiene, advocating for regular data backups, secure internet browsing, and cautious handling of files and attachments. By maintaining a clean and fortified digital environment, individuals can mitigate the risks of privacy breaches and fortify their online resilience.

Digital hygiene serves as the bedrock of online privacy and security. By adopting prudent habits and adhering to best practices, individuals can significantly reduce the vulnerabilities that come with digital interactions. Cultivating a robust digital hygiene routine empowers individuals to take control of their online presence and protect their sensitive information from potential breaches.

Tip 1 Regular Data Backups: Regularly backing up important data is an essential aspect of digital hygiene. By creating duplicate copies of valuable information and storing them in secure locations, individuals can minimize the impact of data loss due to hardware failure, cyberattacks, or accidental deletions. Utilizing cloud storage services or external hard drives provides convenient and reliable options for data backups.

Tip 2 - Secure Internet Browsing: Browsing the internet exposes individuals to various threats, such as malware, phishing attempts, and intrusive tracking mechanisms. Practicing secure internet browsing involves implementing measures to mitigate these risks. Utilizing reputable web browsers, keeping them updated, and installing reliable security extensions or plugins are crucial steps. Additionally, exercising caution when clicking on links, verifying website security (look for the padlock icon and "https" in the URL), and avoiding suspicious or untrusted websites are vital precautions.

Tip 3 - Cautious Handling of Files and Attachments: Files and email attachments can serve as potential vehicles for malware, viruses, or other malicious content. Practicing digital hygiene entails exercising caution when downloading or opening files. Avoid opening attachments from unknown or untrusted sources. Use reliable antivirus software to scan files before opening them. Additionally, be wary of unexpected or unsolicited email attachments, as they may be attempts to deceive or compromise your system.

Tip 4 - Password Hygiene: Maintaining strong and unique passwords is a cornerstone of digital hygiene. Avoid using easily guessable passwords, such as personal information or commonly used words. Instead, opt for lengthy, complex passwords comprising a combination of uppercase and lowercase letters, numbers, and special characters. Employing password managers to generate and securely store passwords ensures convenience without compromising security. Regularly updating passwords and avoiding password reuse across multiple accounts further strengthens digital resilience.

Tip 5 - Software Updates: Keeping software, operating systems, and applications up to date is a critical aspect of digital hygiene. Software updates often include patches and fixes that address security vulnerabilities. Ignoring updates can leave systems susceptible to exploitation. Enabling automatic updates or regularly checking for updates and promptly installing them helps maintain a secure digital environment.

Tip 6 - Privacy Settings and Permissions: Reviewing and adjusting privacy settings across devices, applications, and online platforms is an integral part of digital hygiene. Limiting the information shared and the permissions granted to applications ensures greater control over personal data. Regularly auditing privacy settings and disabling unnecessary data collection or sharing features promotes privacy and minimizes the risk of unintended data exposure.

Cultivating a culture of digital hygiene requires a collective effort to prioritize privacy and security in our daily digital interactions. Organizations and individuals alike must commit to educating themselves and others about the importance of digital hygiene. Integrating digital hygiene practices into our routines and staying updated on emerging threats and best practices ensures that our digital lives remain resilient against evolving risks.

Furthermore, fostering a sense of responsibility and accountability is paramount. Individuals and organizations should prioritize digital hygiene by implementing robust security measures, conducting regular training sessions, and promoting a culture of awareness among employees. By encouraging employees to practice good digital hygiene and providing the necessary resources and support, organizations can establish a strong line of defense against potential cyber threats.

Government agencies and regulatory bodies also play a crucial role in promoting digital hygiene. They can develop and enforce regulations that encourage data protection and privacy, while also providing guidance and resources to educate the public about best practices. Collaboration between public and private sectors is vital in creating a safe digital environment for individuals and businesses alike.

The journey towards maintaining good digital hygiene is ongoing. In a world where our lives are increasingly intertwined with digital technologies, practicing good digital hygiene is no longer optional—it is a fundamental necessity. By adopting practical tips for data backups, secure internet browsing, cautious handling of files and attachments, password hygiene, software updates, and privacy settings, individuals and organizations can fortify their online resilience.

Digital hygiene is a proactive approach to protecting privacy and security in an interconnected world. It requires continuous learning, adaptation, and vigilance. By integrating digital hygiene practices into our daily lives, we can minimize the risk of privacy breaches, safeguard sensitive information, and navigate the online world with confidence.

Ultimately, the responsibility for digital hygiene lies with each individual and organization. By prioritizing privacy, embracing best practices, and fostering a culture of awareness, we can collectively build a resilient digital environment. The Economist magazine stands as a trusted source of information, providing valuable insights and analysis to help readers navigate the evolving challenges of digital hygiene. Together, we can forge a path towards a secure and privacy-conscious digital future.

Empowering Through Education: Nurturing Digital Awareness

This section will explore the significance of education as a powerful tool to navigate the ever-changing privacy risks and best practices. It emphasizes the need for individuals to proactively educate themselves about privacy-related topics through reputable sources, blogs, and online courses. Furthermore, it highlights the value of sharing knowledge and educating others, fostering a collective awareness and promoting responsible digital citizenship.

As technology continues to advance, so do the challenges and risks to our privacy. To protect ourselves effectively, we must commit to ongoing education. By understanding the evolving landscape of digital privacy, we empower ourselves to make informed decisions and adopt practices that safeguard our personal information. Acquiring knowledge about privacy-related topics requires a proactive approach. Individuals should seek out reputable sources that provide reliable and up-to-date information. Reputable news outlets, academic research papers, and established privacy organizations offer valuable insights into the latest privacy risks, emerging technologies, and regulatory developments. Blogs and online forums can also serve as valuable resources, providing real-world experiences and practical advice from privacy experts and individuals with shared interests. Engaging in online communities can foster dialogue and collective learning, enabling individuals to benefit from the experiences and expertise of others.

Online courses and certifications dedicated to privacy and data protection are becoming increasingly prevalent. These educational opportunities provide structured learning experiences, allowing individuals to deepen their understanding of privacy principles, legal frameworks, and best practices. Organizations such as universities, professional associations, and reputable online learning platforms offer a range of courses catering to various levels of expertise.

Education is not solely for personal benefit—it has the power to create a ripple effect by empowering others and fostering a culture of responsible digital citizenship. Sharing knowledge about privacy-related topics with friends, family, colleagues, and broader communities can raise awareness and drive positive change. Engaging in open discussions, hosting workshops or webinars, and participating in community events provide opportunities to disseminate knowledge and address common misconceptions about privacy. By sharing insights, best practices, and emerging privacy concerns, individuals can help others understand the importance of privacy and take proactive steps to protect their digital lives.

Promoting responsible digital citizenship also involves educating younger generations about privacy from an early age. Schools, parents, and educational institutions should integrate privacy education into curricula, teaching children and young adults about the importance of online privacy, the potential risks they may encounter, and how to make informed decisions regarding their personal information.

Collective efforts are key to driving positive change in the realm of digital privacy. Collaboration among individuals, privacy advocates, technology companies, policymakers, and civil society organizations is essential. By joining forces, these stakeholders can advocate for stronger privacy protections, push for transparent data practices, and shape policies that prioritize individual rights and data security. Furthermore, active engagement with policymakers and participation in public consultations and advocacy campaigns can influence privacy regulations and promote responsible data practices at a systemic level. Encouraging transparency and accountability from technology companies, advocating for user-centric design, and promoting privacy-by-design principles are important steps towards a more privacy-conscious digital ecosystem.

Continual learning and education are foundational pillars of digital privacy protection. By actively seeking knowledge from reliable sources, engaging in online courses, and sharing insights with others, individuals can become informed and responsible guardians of their digital lives. Education not only empowers individuals to make informed decisions but also fosters collective awareness and drives positive change at both personal and societal levels.

The importance of education extends beyond personal empowerment. By sharing knowledge and educating others, we contribute to a broader culture of responsible digital citizenship. It is through collective awareness and action that we can shape a more privacy-conscious and secure world.

Collaboration and advocacy are crucial elements of promoting privacy initiatives. By working together with privacy advocates, technology companies, policymakers, and civil society organizations, we can amplify our voices and advocate for stronger privacy protections. Through collaborative efforts, we can influence policy changes, push for transparent data practices, and ensure that privacy remains a top priority in the digital realm.

Engaging with policymakers and participating in public consultations and advocacy campaigns provides opportunities to shape privacy regulations and influence the direction of data protection practices. By advocating for user-centric design and privacy-by-design principles, we can foster an environment where privacy is not an afterthought but an integral part of every digital product and service.

Education is a powerful tool in the pursuit of privacy and digital security. By continually learning about privacy-related topics, accessing reliable sources of information, and engaging in educational opportunities, we empower ourselves to navigate the evolving landscape with confidence. Moreover, by sharing our knowledge, educating others, and actively participating in collaborative efforts and advocacy, we contribute to a culture of responsible digital citizenship and help shape a more privacy-conscious and secure future for all.

Some excellent and easy to access media for educating oneself on the basics of online privacy issues are listed below. These sources also provide more advanced content.

Online courses

1. https://www.harvardonline.harvard.edu/course/data-privacy-technology
2. https://www.coursera.org/learn/data-security-privacy
3. https://www.edx.org/learn/data-privacy
4. https://www.open.edu/openlearn/mod/oucontent/view.php?id=50885
5. https://www.eccouncil.org/cybersecurity-exchange/cyber-novice/free-cybersecurity-courses-beginners/

Some excellent web sites providing best practices

1. https://www.npr.org/2020/10/09/922262686/your-technology-is-tracking-you-take-these-steps-for-better-online-privacy
2. https://discoverprivacy.com/privacy-fundamentals/ultimate-guide-to-protecting-personal-information-online/
3. https://proton.me/blog/how-to-protect-personal-information-online
4. https://www.pcmag.com/picks/essential-apps-for-protecting-your-privacy-online
5. https://consumer.ftc.gov/consumer-alerts/2021/06/your-guide-protecting-your-privacy-online

YouTube channels to subscribe to

1. https://www.youtube.com/@AllThingsSecured
2. https://www.youtube.com/@davidbombal
3. https://www.youtube.com/@NaomiBrockwellTV
4. https://www.youtube.com/@robbraxmantech
5. https://www.youtube.com/@LironSegev

In today's world, protecting personal privacy requires a proactive approach and a heightened level of awareness. By adopting strategies such as utilizing encryption tools, being cautious about sharing information, employing strong passwords and two-factor authentication, regularly updating software, and utilizing VPNs, individuals can enhance their online privacy and reduce the risk of privacy breaches. Furthermore, cultivating privacy awareness through self education is crucial for responsible digital citizenship. Understanding the implications of online activities, practicing digital hygiene, and educating oneself and others contribute to a more informed and empowered approach to privacy protection. By implementing these strategies and fostering privacy awareness, individuals can assert greater control over their personal information, mitigate privacy risks, and make informed decisions in the digital realm. However, it is essential to acknowledge that privacy is a dynamic landscape, constantly influenced by technological advancements and evolving threats. Therefore, ongoing vigilance, adaptability, and a commitment to staying informed are paramount.

This section has provided practical advice on protecting privacy in the digital realm through strategies such as encryption tools, cautious information sharing, strong passwords, software updates, and VPN usage. Additionally, it has emphasized the importance of privacy awareness in understanding the implications of online activities and practicing responsible digital citizenship. By incorporating these strategies into their digital lives and continuously educating themselves, individuals can navigate the risks with greater confidence and safeguard their personal information. In an environment where privacy is increasingly valued and threatened, empowering individuals to protect their privacy becomes not only a personal responsibility but also a fundamental pillar of a secure and ethical digital society.

Chapter 9
Online Marketing and Tracking

"The Internet is the first thing that humanity has built that humanity doesn't understand, the largest experiment in anarchy that we have ever had."

Eric Schmidt, former CEO of Google

To visit a website, your browser sends a request to that website when you visit it. Despite this, additional advertising codes and invisible trackers may be hidden behind the scenes on the website. These codes cause your browser to make numerous requests to third-party websites that are not visible to you. Your browser and user information is contained in these requests, such as your time zone, browser settings, and the versions of software installed on your computer. This is similar to walking into a store and not realizing that a surveillance camera records your every move. Although you cannot see it, your actions are tracked and monitored in excruciating detail. This data is then used to create a profile of you that can be used to target ads and other content to you specifically.

Over time and multiple websites, this profile can be built up to the point where third-party data brokers sell it. Data on social media sites is also often augmented to this profile. This data can manipulate you into taking specific actions, such as buying certain products or visiting certain websites. It can also be used to create false narratives about you, which can have severe implications regarding privacy and security. For example, a data broker may have access to your browsing habits, purchase history, and even your location and use this information to create a false narrative that you are a terrorist or a criminal. This false narrative can then be sold to third parties, who can use it to take action against you, such as denying you access to certain services or even blacklisting you. While the exact percentage is unknown, it is estimated that 80% or more users have had at least some of their personal information sold by a Data Broker. It's like there is an underground marketplace for personal information, where your information is sold in a highly profitable and primarily unregulated manner. It's like entering a dark alley where a few people are making money off unsuspecting victims. This type of tracking can be challenging to detect and has profound implications for digital privacy. For example, a recent study found that out of the 1,000 top websites in the United States, 87 per cent use tracking technology to collect personal data without the user's knowledge. As author Greg Bear once wrote in science fiction, "To fight an enemy properly, you have to know what they are. Ignorance is defeat." While some of this information is necessary for viewing the page, a lot of it is collected by third-party ad networks. These networks use sneaky tracking mechanisms across the Internet to gather your information. Though the data points may seem insignificant, they can create a detailed online activity profile combined. This includes your education level, income bracket, and political affiliation. Your online activity can be logged as long as this data remains linked to you. Ad networks typically use cookie tracking and browser fingerprinting to maintain this link. What are cookies? For example, if you click on a link to a news article from a particular political party, this could be used to infer your political affiliation.

Cookies are small chunks of information that websites store in your browser. Their primary use is remembering helpful things like your account login info or what items were in your online shopping cart—in other words, and they save your place. But they can also be misused to link all your visits, searches, and other activities on a site together. Cookies are a privacy violation, and browsers generally allow you to block, limit, or delete cookies. However, some websites need cookies to function correctly. Blocking them can cause the site to malfunction. Awareness of the risks and weighing the pros and cons of using cookies is essential. For instance, if a user has blocked cookies, they may be unable to access certain parts of a website or may receive an error message when attempting to proceed, such as "Cookie permission required."

A digital fingerprint lists a user's unique characteristics, browser, and hardware setup. This includes information the browser needs to send to access websites, like the location of the website the user is requesting. But it also includes seemingly insignificant data (like screen resolution and installed fonts) gathered by tracking scripts. Tracking sites can stitch all the small pieces together to form a unique picture, or "fingerprint," of your device.

The difference between these techniques is subtle but important to understand. Consider the small tracking devices scientists use to follow animal migration patterns or a GPS transmitter attached to a car. As long as they're attached to the target animal or vehicle, they are accurate and effective—but they lose all value if they're knocked off or discarded. This is roughly how cookies work: they track users until they are deleted.

Fingerprinting uses more permanent identifiers, such as hardware specifications and browser settings. This is equivalent to tracking a bird by its song or feather markings or a car by its license plate, make, model, and color. In other words, metrics that are challenging to change and impossible to delete. Fingerprints usually contain a device's OS, screen size, and time zone are all factors that can be used to create a unique fingerprint for tracking purposes.

Blocking trackers is difficult, even with a fully-featured tracker blocker. To protect your online privacy and prevent tracking, you can use browser extensions to block cookies, delete your browsing history, and use private browsing modes. You can also limit the amount of personal information you share online and be careful about the links you click on. Privacy protection does not have to be perfect to make a big difference!

Two central dynamics make trackers challenging to avoid online:

Impact on Usability: Unfortunately, enhanced privacy often comes at the expense of functionality. For instance, you may disable JavaScript to stop tracking scripts from running. But this will likely make shopping, filling out forms, watching videos, or seeing interactive web elements more difficult. Many pages require turning off your ad blocker to see content or refuse to load anything unless you use the "official" app.

Identifiable Protections: Your protections can become part of your fingerprint. An add-on intended to protect you can even identify you. Changing your settings and installing protections can prevent trackers from being identified. In this case, you become a "mystery user with a specific combination of privacy protections installed."

To protect your online identity, consider using browser extensions to block cookies, secure HTTPS connections, virtual private networks (VPNs) to hide IP addresses, and two-factor authentication (2FA) for added security. Additionally, you can limit the amount of personal information you share online, be mindful of the links you click on, and use private browsing modes to protect your identity further. You can also create multiple online identities to protect yourself further. For example, you can use different usernames, email addresses, and passwords for different accounts and websites. This way, if one of your identities is compromised, others will remain secure.

Additionally, you can use Proton Mail and other encrypted mail providers to protect your emails and email generators for various sites linked to your real email account, such as SimpleLogin. This creates a set of secure logins that are difficult to hack. Using these services, you can further protect your personal information and keep it from falling into the wrong hands. Additionally, you should regularly monitor your accounts for unauthorized activity and be aware of the latest security threats to protect yourself. You can also use virtual phone numbers for added security. Virtual phone numbers are separate numbers from your actual phone number, which you can use to verify your accounts or to sign up for services without revealing your personal information. Setting up a virtual phone number on your phone is easy. You can use apps like Google Voice and Burner to create a virtual phone number and link it to your existing phone number. This allows you to receive and make calls without revealing your personal information. You can also use virtual phone numbers to create virtual credit cards linked to your real-world credit card. This can help protect your financial information when shopping online, as virtual credit cards can be turned on or off, have limits applied to them in terms of available funds, or are only connected to a single store and not usable on other shopping sites. For example, a virtual credit card can only be set up to pay monthly Netflix subscriptions. If the virtual card number is compromised or stolen, it is of little use to the thief as it can't be used elsewhere and can quickly be cancelled by you, thus protecting your identity and the linkage back to your real-world card number. Finally, using a secure network when accessing the Internet is essential. Make sure you use strong passwords and two-factor authentication to protect your accounts. Keep track of your monthly expenses to ensure that any suspicious activity can be detected quickly. Lastly, constantly monitor your credit reports for any unauthorized activity.

Tor Browser is the most realistic protection currently available for browsers, which has reduced browser fingerprint ability. For day-to-day use, the best options are to run tools like Privacy Badger or Disconnect, which will block some (but unfortunately not all) of the domains that try to perform fingerprinting, and to use a tool like NoScript (for Firefox), which significantly reduces the amount of data available to fingerprinters.

Cover Your Tracks' primary goal is to help you determine the balance between privacy and convenience. By summarizing your overall protection and a list of characteristics that make up your digital fingerprint, you can see exactly how your browser appears to trackers. You can also see how implementing different protection methods changes this visibility. The following suggestions are simple, straightforward protection methods with excellent starting points.

Chapter 10

The Future of Privacy and Surveillance

"Good name in man and woman, dear my lord,
Is the immediate jewel of their souls:
Who steals my purse steals trash; 'tis something, nothing;
'Twas mine, 'tis his, and has been slave to thousands:
But he that filches from me my good name
Robs me of that which not enriches him
And makes me poor indeed."

- William Shakespeare, Othello

In an age where technology reigns supreme and the boundaries of privacy are constantly under siege, the future of privacy and surveillance presents a daunting prospect. This landscape is constantly changing and it is sometimes daunting to try and keep up. Still there are very much identifiable trends and in examining these we can craft a personal privacy strategy for ourselves. This chapter aims to assist in that process.

There is no doubt the ubiquitous reach of surveillance technology is expanding like a voracious beast. Smart devices, facial recognition algorithms, and data analytics enable unprecedented access to personal information, forever altering the relationship between privacy and power. Governments and corporations are now the custodians of our most intimate details, raising concerns about mass surveillance, data breaches, and the erosion of individual autonomy. The future of surveillance looms before us, draped in the garb of artificial intelligence, biometrics, and predictive analytics—a world where privacy teeters on the edge of extinction.

In this turbulent landscape, the fight for privacy intensifies. As the clamor for data protection grows, regulatory responses have emerged in an attempt to stem the tide of intrusion. The European Union's General Data Protection Regulation (GDPR) and California's Consumer Privacy Act (CCPA) have embarked upon a treacherous path, aiming to safeguard individual privacy in an increasingly connected world. Yet, let us not be naïve, for these measures are but the tip of the iceberg, grappling with the profound challenges of jurisdictional differences, global data flows, and the ever-elusive nature of technology that perpetually outpaces the flimsy armory of legislative action.

Technological innovations, forged in the crucible of necessity, possess the potential to revive individual privacy. Blockchain, encryption, and decentralized systems hold the promise of restoring power to the people, granting them the ability to reclaim control over their personal data. With zero-knowledge proofs and differential privacy techniques, individuals can once again dance on the edge of anonymity, armed

As we traverse this treacherous landscape, ethics and transparency must serve as our guiding beacons. Technological advancements, divorced from ethical considerations, threaten to plunge us further into the abyss. Transparency in data collection and usage practices is our lifeline—a pledge of trust between individuals and the entities that seek to pry into their lives. The principles of privacy by design and default, coupled with stringent security measures, must underpin the foundations of our technological edifices. Only through the relentless pursuit of ethical principles and unwavering transparency can we hope to navigate this perilous horizon.

At the crux of this predicament lies the Faustian bargain—the delicate trade-off between security and individual privacy. Governments, burdened with the solemn duty to protect, tread a treacherous path where civil liberties hang in the balance. Striking the right balance demands a rigorous examination of the symbiotic relationship between security measures and the sanctity of personal autonomy. Ongoing dialogue, rigorous oversight, and unwavering transparency must guide our decisions as we attempt to redefine the social contract at a time when surveillance and privacy intertwine.

Privacy and surveillance have become increasingly intertwined,, as technological advancements continue to shape the way we interact, communicate, and share information. The future of privacy holds both promises and challenges, as new technologies offer potential solutions to enhance privacy while the need to balance it with security persists. We will now turn to focusing on three key aspects: the potential for new technologies to enhance privacy, the ongoing challenges of striking a balance between privacy and security, and the importance of privacy activism in advocating for stronger privacy protections.

New technologies and privacy

With the rapid development of new technologies, privacy and security are poised to undergo a revolution never seen before. Blockchain, a decentralized, immutable ledger system, exemplifies this potential. A blockchain-enabled individual can secure their data and limit access to it to authorized parties by harnessing its power. Blockchain's transparent yet secure nature empowers individuals to safeguard their privacy in the digital world. For example, blockchain technology can be used to store medical records in a, secure, immutable way and accessible only to those with permission to view the data. This ensures that no one can access a person's medical records without consent. Moreover, blockchain-based systems enable individuals to have complete control over their data. This makes it possible for them to choose who can access it and what information can be shared.

As well as enhancing privacy, decentralized systems can reduce risks associated with single points of failure—for example, unauthorized access by distributing data across multiple nodes. As a result of decentralization, individuals are granted ownership over their data, addressing privacy concerns associated with centralized data storage and surveillance.

Furthermore, new technologies such as homomorphic encryption and zero-knowledge proofs facilitate secure data computations and transactions without revealing the data. These advances could revolutionize the way financial transactions and healthcare data sharing are conducted. Homomorphic encryption is a type of encryption that allows computations to be done on data without decrypting it. It works by encrypting data with two different keys, one for encryption and one for decryption, and then allowing computations to be done on the encrypted data. This technology would allow for secure computing and data sharing without compromising the original data. It could also protect sensitive data from unauthorized users accessing or modifying it. This would significantly impact the finance, healthcare, and government industries. Zero-knowledge proofs are a type of cryptography that allows for secure communication without revealing any underlying data. This technology can be used to verify information without revealing the data itself. It proves that the person or system making the claim owns the data without revealing it.

The good news is that the tools and technologies that drive digital transformation, when used responsibly and ethically, can foster trust among stakeholders and yield societal benefits. Further, they can be used to prevent adverse events such as data breaches and boost trust. Digital tools and technologies can be positive enablers of transformation and trust when used to enhance transparency, reinforce ethical practices, bolster data privacy, and strengthen security.

Aspect 1: Transparent accessibility

It is becoming increasingly common for stakeholders to expect organizations to be more transparent as digital products and services increase. The consumer has access to a wealth of information online before interacting with digital platforms, not only about the products and services they are interested in but also about the companies offering them. As we have seen in this book, companies often collect personal and confidential information from consumers in return. Their expectations include transparency regarding the storage, use, and application of artificial intelligence (AI) and decision-making tools. In a survey, most Americans believe that business transparency is more important than ever, with many willing to pay for products that guarantee complete transparency. The survey found that 86% of respondents believe that transparency in business is more important now than ever.

Organizations must embrace transparency and accessibility to compete in the digital world. There are numerous "business practices" to accomplish this:

Practice 1.1 - One way for organizations to improve their credibility is by implementing transparency measures on their digital platforms. This can include clearly labelling sponsored or promotional content and separating voluntary reviews from verified purchasers. By doing so, customers can more easily evaluate the company and its offerings.

Practice 1.2 - It's important for organizations to make their products and services easy to understand. This can be done by using conversational interfaces that simplify complex terms into everyday language. Additionally, providing on-demand helpdesks through various channels can give customers the confidence they need to make informed decisions.

Practice 1.3 - Explainable AI (XAI) technologies can promote confidence in the recommended outcome. For example in a medical diagnosis, XAI technologies are excellent at explaining the probability and contribution of each patient symptom, which can help build confidence in AI-supported medical diagnoses for the consumer. This transparency can be especially beneficial for patients who may be skeptical of relying on technology for their healthcare needs. It's important to remember that these technologies are here to support medical professionals and provide additional insights, not replace them.

Practice 1.4 - Manufacturers and logistics companies can use blockchain technologies to track production sources and handling conditions, easing concerns about safety, sustainability, authenticity, and more.

Aspect 2 - Ethical responsibility

Despite technology's many wonders, there is also a dark side, as we have seen, that requires ethical consideration. Ethical considerations become critical since technology's logic may not align with human notions of right and wrong. For example, AI-driven facial recognition technology can identify and track people, leading to serious ethical questions about privacy and data security. Companies must evaluate how technology aligns with their purpose and core principles to address customer needs, foster fairness, inclusion, and well-being, and curb disinformation. An organization's alignment with its purpose and core principles provides a basis for consumers to evaluate if their data is being used responsibly and ethically. They must consider the potential risks and consequences of using technology and ensure that it is not creating any unintended negative impacts.

As far as ethics and responsibility are concerned, companies can do the following:

Practice 2.1 - Utilizing technology to triage consumer complaints ensures urgent and complex concerns receive human attention by ironing out complaints in a sensitive and timely manner. Sentiment analysis, for example, can help identify urgent complaints, while computer vision technologies can help insurance companies assess damage.

Practice 2.2 - Combating spoofing, deepfakes, and rumors: Digital solutions can be employed to verify and debunk suspicious messages.

Practice 2.3 - In law enforcement, higher education, and the criminal justice system, organizations can adopt algorithms that identify and minimize unintended harm by using fairness-testing tools.

Practice 2.4 Preventing unhealthy or irresponsible user engagement by implementing safeguards for stakeholder welfare and responsible technology use: Prevention measures can prevent unhealthy or irresponsible user engagement. A content aggregator may warn users about the integrity of crowdsourced information or limit time and spend on habit-forming games.

Aspect 3 - Control

Although individuals have freely traded data for convenience and personalized experiences over the years, consent is usually conditional and limited. When consumers think their data is being misused or mishandled, they call for boycotts, inquiries, and penalties under privacy laws. However, a survey finds that individuals are willing to share their data if they perceive its benefits.

Organizations can adopt the following approaches to encourage safe data sharing and control:

Practice 3.1 - Offering privacy dashboards that allow users to monitor data collection, usage, and retention empowers consumers. Some companies even enable redaction, deletion, or transfer of data to alternative providers.

Practice 3.2 - Organizations are turning to "zero-party data" collected directly from consumers to ensure accurate and personalized services rather than relying on outdated or inferred third-party data.

Practice 3.3 - Technology advancements enable organizations to analyze encrypted customer data without decrypting it. Privacy-preserving techniques like on-device data analysis provide an alternative approach.

Aspect 4 - Reliable security

An organization's cybersecurity record significantly influences consumers' decisions regarding engaging with its services. Consumers value the convenience of digital technologies but expect their organizations to take responsibility for the security of their data and the privacy of their online users.

Organizations can take the following steps to ensure security and reliability:

Practice 4.1 - Verifying identity to reduce impersonation and fraud: Multifactor authentication or digital biometrics, which identify customers based on their online behavior, make the experience more frictionless. Verification measures include cursor movements, keystroke speed, and voice recognition.

Practice 4.2 - Automation and artificial intelligence can reduce human errors, process vast information, and detect anomalies that humans might miss. Secure chatbots and AI-based fraud detection tools are examples of such automation and AI processes.

Practice 4.3 Alerting users to suspicious account activity: Intelligent threat detection tools can alert users to unusual logins or significant transactions in their accounts, encouraging proactive security measures.

The evolution of privacy and surveillance requires us to recognize the potential of new technologies to enhance privacy whilst also understanding the ongoing challenges of balancing privacy with security. Here again, privacy activism is critical in advocating for stronger protections. This complex landscape involves individuals, government, and responsible technological innovation interplay. A future that upholds individual privacy while benefiting from technological advancements can be ensured by responsibly embracing digital tools and technologies, addressing challenges with balance, and fostering a culture of privacy activism.

I truly believe we are at a the crossroads as a society, the future of privacy and surveillance is like all things, uncertain. The intricate interplay between technology, legislation, ethics, and societal expectations will shape the trajectory of our privacy rights. No doubt the road ahead is strewn with challenges, but through collaboration, innovation, and unyielding dedication to individual liberties, we may yet chart a course that upholds privacy as a fundamental pillar of our democratic ideals in this digital epoch. It is a battle worth fighting—a battle to safeguard against the possibility of an ever-encroaching surveillance state.

Chapter 11

Political Movements for Privacy: Advocacy, History, Current Movements, and Individual Involvement

"An ounce of prevention is worth a pound of cure."

Benjamin Franklin

Privacy is a fundamental right that has increasingly come under threat in recent decades. We now turn to that important tool we have in our societies, political action. In many ways it is our most effective and cherished tool. My objective in this chapter is to cultivate a sense of the significance of political action in driving transformational change, the history of privacy activism, current political movements for privacy, and practical ways individuals can get involved. By exploring these aspects, we gain a deeper understanding of the role of political movements in advocating for privacy protections and the fundamentally transformative role it can play over when applied with pressure, numbers and over time.

Political action plays a crucial role in protecting privacy rights. There are a number of ways that this can take form, for example advocacy groups, grassroots movements, and political parties. Nevertheless, such mechanisms should be considered in light of the objectives, to raise awareness, shape public opinion, and change policy decisions for the better. In doing so, political action naturally promotes transparency, and accountability. All three of which are needed in the enactment of privacy-focused legislation.

With the advent of increasingly sophisticated, miniaturized, and distributed technologies, personal information is gathered, processed, and disseminated in a bewildering variety of ways: identity cards, biometrics, video surveillance, cookies, spyware, data mining, profiling, and many more. People and groups worldwide have challenged the most intrusive surveillance practices of governments and corporations.

We will now examine the landmark court cases and legislative victories that have shaped the landscape of privacy rights over the past century. Understanding the evolution and importance of privacy protections in our society is enhanced when we trace the roots of privacy activism to pivotal historical events and examine the contributions of influential privacy advocates.

Sparks of awareness

The U.S. Constitution does not explicitly protect privacy, despite the importance of it in our everyday lives. U.S. courts have relied on protections articulated in the Bill of Rights, such as the Fourth Amendment, in resolving privacy disputes. This Amendment prohibits unreasonable searches and seizures. Due to the lack of specific constitutional privacy protections, judicial opinions have conflicted, and the public needs clarification (although recent developments explored below have gone someway towards providing clarification). As an early guidepost through this thicket, Samuel Warren and Louis Brandeis published an article in the Harvard Law Review in 1890 arguing that privacy protections are part of a "right to be let alone." Over the following decades, the article influenced privacy theories and has been cited in vital Supreme Court decisions.

However, society has undergone profound changes since the 19th century. Today, we are surrounded by technologies that track our behavior and communications, capture our data for targeted advertising, trade it among data brokerages, and mine it for criminal and political purposes. This influential work argued for recognizing the right to be left alone and free from unwarranted intrusion at a time when the right to be left alone is more under threat than ever. This article captured the essence of privacy and laid the foundation for future legal arguments and activism.

Landmark Court Cases

Privacy activism found its way into courtrooms, where significant legal battles were fought to establish and defend privacy rights. One landmark case that reshaped our understanding of privacy was Katz v. United States in 1967. Acting on a suspicion that Katz was transmitting gambling information to clients elsewhere in the country over the phone, Federal agents attached an eavesdropping device to the outside of a public phone booth used by Katz. Based on the recordings of his conversations, Katz was convicted under an eight-count indictment for the illegal transmission of wagering information from Los Angeles to Boston and Miami. Katz challenged his conviction on appeal, arguing that the recordings were unconstitutionally obtained and, therefore, could not be used as evidence against him. The Court of Appeals rejected this point, noting the absence of a physical intrusion into the phone booth itself. The critical question the Supreme Court had to consider was, "Does the Fourth Amendment protection against unreasonable searches and seizures require the authorities to obtain a search warrant to wiretap a public pay phone?"

The Court ruled that Katz was entitled to Fourth Amendment protection and that this covered his conversations. It was ruled that a physical intrusion into the area he occupied was unnecessary to make the Amendment relevant in the context. "The Fourth Amendment protects people, not places," wrote Justice Stewart for the Supreme Court. The Supreme Court, in this case, held that the Fourth Amendment protection against unreasonable searches and seizures extended to an individual's reasonable expectation of privacy, even in public spaces. This decision set a precedent that privacy rights were not confined to physical spaces alone but also extended to personal communications and activities.

The landmark case of Griswold v. Connecticut (1965) profoundly impacted privacy law and legislation. A Connecticut law criminalized contraceptives, even for married couples. As a result of the Supreme Court's ruling in favor of Griswold and her colleagues, the law was struck down, and a constitutional right to privacy was established.

Justice William O. Douglas, writing for the Supreme Court, emphasized that specific constitutional provisions, such as the First, Third, Fourth, Fifth, and Ninth Amendments, protect people's liberties against unwarranted government intrusion. Although the Constitution does not explicitly mention a right to privacy, the Court recognized that it is derived from the penumbras and emanations of these explicit guarantees.

As a result of Griswold v. Connecticut, privacy rights in intimate matters were recognized for the first time. According to the Court, the law violated the right to marital privacy, affirming that married couples have a fundamental right to choose contraception without government interference. Future reproductive rights cases, including Roe v. Wade (1973), which legalized abortion nationwide, were influenced by this recognition of marital privacy.

Second, the Griswold ruling had broader implications for privacy rights. By acknowledging that the Constitution protects a right to privacy, the Court opened the door for future cases to explore and expand privacy protections in various contexts. Subsequent cases, such as Roe v. Wade, Lawrence v. Texas, and others, relied on the reasoning and framework established in Griswold to further recognize and protect privacy rights in matters of personal autonomy, sexual conduct, and family decision-making.

Beyond its impact on case law, Griswold v. Connecticut also influenced legislative efforts to protect privacy rights. In response to the ruling, several states repealed or amended laws restricting contraceptive access, aligning their statutes with the constitutional right to privacy. The decision spurred public discourse and led to legislation protecting privacy in other areas, such as medical decisions, data protection, and surveillance practices.

Another landmark case on privacy was Lawrence v. Texas (2003), and it had a significant impact on privacy case law and legislation, particularly in the context of LGBTQ+ rights. The case challenged a Texas law that criminalized consensual sexual activity between same-sex individuals. The Supreme Court's ruling in Lawrence v. Texas struck down the Texas law and established a broader recognition of privacy rights and equality under the law. In the majority opinion, Justice Anthony Kennedy wrote that the Texas law violated the Due Process Clause of the Fourteenth Amendment, which protects individuals' fundamental rights to liberty and privacy. The Court held that the state's intrusion into the private sexual conduct of consenting adults, regardless of their sexual orientation, violated their constitutional rights.

The impact of Lawrence v. Texas on privacy case law was twofold. First, it recognized that adults have a fundamental right to engage in private sexual conduct, consensual, without government interference. The ruling expanded the scope of privacy rights beyond intimate decisions within the marital context, as previously established in cases like Griswold v. Connecticut and Roe v. Wade, to encompass the sexual autonomy and personal choices of all individuals. Second, the case had broader implications for LGBTQ+ rights and equal protection under the law. By striking down the Texas law, the Court effectively invalidated similar laws criminalizing same-sex sexual activity in other states. The decision set a precedent that laws targeting individuals based on sexual orientation were unconstitutional and violated equal protection principles. The case extended beyond case law and influenced legislative efforts to protect privacy and LGBTQ+ rights. The ruling prompted states to reevaluate and repeal their laws criminalizing consensual same-sex sexual activity. It provided momentum for the broader movement towards LGBTQ+ equality, leading to advancements in marriage equality, anti-discrimination laws, and other legal protections for LGBTQ+ individuals. Lawrence v. Texas also had a global impact, serving as a persuasive authority for courts and advocates worldwide. The decision contributed to the global trend toward decriminalizing same-sex sexual activity and influenced the advancement of LGBTQ+ rights in other countries.

Finally, Carpenter v. United States (2018) is a landmark case that has significantly impacted privacy case law, particularly regarding digital privacy and the Fourth Amendment. The case involved law enforcement collecting historical cell phone location data without a warrant. The Supreme Court's ruling in Carpenter v. United States established new guidelines for protecting individuals' privacy. In the case, the Court grappled with whether obtaining historical cell phone location data constituted a search under the Fourth Amendment and required a warrant supported by probable cause. The Court departed from the traditional understanding that individuals have no reasonable expectation of privacy in information voluntarily shared with third parties, such as cell phone providers. The Court's opinion, written by Chief Justice Roberts, held that accessing cell phone historical data about locations and times constitutes a search under the Fourth Amendment. The Court reasoned that individuals expect privacy in their physical movements and that collecting extensive, detailed location data over an extended period implicates privacy interests. Therefore, obtaining such data without a warrant violates the Fourth Amendment's protection against unreasonable searches and seizures.

The impact of Carpenter v. United States on privacy case law has been profound, particularly in the context of digital surveillance and data privacy. The ruling recognized that the digital footprints we leave behind, such as cell phone location data, can reveal sensitive information about our private lives and activities. It underscored the need for stronger privacy protections in the and shifted the legal landscape by acknowledging that traditional notions of privacy must adapt to evolving technology. Following the Carpenter decision, lower courts have relied on its reasoning to evaluate the constitutionality of other forms of digital surveillance and data collection. The ruling has prompted courts to scrutinize the collection of digital information, such as email communications, internet browsing history, and social media data, and assess whether individuals reasonably expect privacy in these areas. This important ruling has spurred legislative discussions and efforts to update privacy laws to reflect the realities of the digital era. It has fueled debates about the need for comprehensive data protection legislation and increased transparency and accountability in government surveillance practices. The ruling has also expanded the understanding of the Fourth Amendment's protections to encompass digital information and set a precedent for evaluating the constitutionality of government surveillance and data collection practices. Its impact extends beyond the specific case, shaping the legal framework surrounding digital privacy and laying the groundwork for continued discussions on balancing privacy rights with law enforcement interests. These cases represent significant milestones in developing privacy law and have had a lasting impact on the interpretation and protection of privacy rights in the United States. It is important to note that privacy law varies across different jurisdictions, and landmark cases may differ in other countries.

Privacy activism has also been instrumental in developing and implementing privacy laws. One notable example is the European Union's General Data Protection Regulation (GDPR). Enforced in 2018, the GDPR marked a significant milestone in privacy advocacy by providing a comprehensive framework for data protection and privacy rights. It introduced strict guidelines for how organizations collect, process, and store personal data, ensuring greater transparency and control for individuals over their information. The GDPR influenced European countries and inspired privacy activists worldwide to advocate for similar legislation in their jurisdictions.

Privacy advocates and milestones

Numerous privacy advocates have played a crucial role in shaping privacy rights discourse and achievements throughout history. One such figure is Alan Westin, whose seminal work "Privacy and Freedom", published in 1967, explored the interplay between privacy, technology, and individual autonomy. Westin's scholarship and advocacy efforts helped raise public consciousness about the potential dangers of unchecked surveillance and catalyzed privacy activism.

In recent years, the revelations by Edward Snowden regarding mass surveillance programs have further fueled the urgency for privacy protections. Snowden's whistleblowing activities shed light on the extensive surveillance conducted by governments and private entities, prompting widespread debate and mobilizing privacy activists worldwide. The ensuing public discourse led to increased scrutiny of surveillance practices, calls for transparency, and the strengthening of privacy rights through legal reforms.

Legislative victories

Throughout privacy activism, legislative victories have played a crucial role in fortifying privacy rights and establishing new safeguards. This section explores notable legislative successes achieved by privacy advocates in the United States and worldwide. In addition to the passage of the Electronic Communications Privacy Act (ECPA) in 1986, there is a patchwork but nevertheless significant privacy-related legislation, that has strengthened privacy rights and at least partially addressed emerging challenges. We are not starting from zero.

Some history first. In the 1980s, and in the US, as electronic communications became increasingly prevalent, and as a consequence so did concerns regarding the privacy of these digital interactions. The existing legal frameworks in most democratic countries did not adequately address the unique challenges posed by emerging technologies, leaving individuals vulnerable to unwarranted surveillance. Recognizing the need to update privacy laws, lawmakers across the world sought to bridge this gap and provide legal protections for electronic communications. With different levels of enthusiasm and from different starring points.

In the United States, and in response to these growing concerns, Congress passed, in 1986, the Electronic Communications Privacy Act (ECPA). The ECPA represented a significant stride forward in protecting the privacy of electronic communications, and the Act amended the existing and somewhat ancient wiretap laws. The Act also extended legal protections to various forms of electronic communication, including emails, voicemails, and electronic messages.

One of the key provisions of the ECPA was the requirement for law enforcement agencies to obtain a warrant based on probable cause[180]. This was strictly required before accessing electronic communications, and as we shall see had become the fundamental principle that is most under threat today. This safeguard aimed to balance the needs of law enforcement with the preservation of privacy rights, ensuring that individuals' communications were not subject to arbitrary and invasive surveillance. Importantly it is also enshrine in the US constitution no less[181].

The passage of the ECPA marked an important legislative victory for privacy rights in the United States. By explicitly recognizing the need for privacy protections in electronic communications, the ECPA acknowledged the evolving landscape of technology and the importance of safeguarding individuals' privacy in accordance with the founding constitutional documents. The ECPA established a clear legal framework for protecting these electronic communications, offering individuals a reasonable expectation of privacy in their digital interactions. It provided essential safeguards against unwarranted surveillance and was a crucial tool for individuals, organizations, and service providers to defend their privacy rights. However one major concern with the legislation was that it did not explicitly protect actions such as Sending an email or another kind of message online. This requires the user to give information to a company that transfers, processes, and holds the user's information. The principle known as the *third-party doctrine[182] and it* held that the Fourth Amendment generally does not protect private information shared with third parties. Thus large amounts of data in the modern world generated by digital activities are effectively moving through the infrastructure and servers of third parties and hence most governments have relied on the third party doctrine to defend their excessive collection and screening of large populations. In the event that courts continue to take the third-party doctrine seriously, police could lawfully obtain all of this information without a warrant or probable cause. Even one's mere curiosity can and will be monitored, and this is not hyperbole. The state of affairs poses one of the most significant threats to privacy in the 21st century, according to Daniel Solove[183].

---

[180] https://law.justia.com/constitution/us/amendment-04/08-probable-cause.html

[181] Fourth amendment reads "The right of the people to be secure in their persons, houses, papers, and effects, against unreasonable searches and seizures, shall not be violated, and no Warrants shall issue but upon probable cause, supported by Oath or affirmation, and particularly describing the place to be searched, and the persons or things to be seized."

[182] https://crsreports.congress.gov/product/pdf/LSB/LSB10801

[183] Daniel J. Solove, Digital Dossiers and the Dissipation of Fourth Amendment Privacy, 75 S. CAL. L. REV. 1083, 1087 (2002)

We now now live in a world where nearly every call or click online leaves a digital trail that can be stored, searched, and stitched together to reveal an intimate portrait of private lives. However, the current law in most jurisdictions provides little privacy protection for information about these activities, and in the US it undermines the First and Fourth Amendment safeguards for US citizens that are essential to a robust democracy. Among the most prominent critics of the rule is Justice Sotomayor, who has described the rule as "ill suited to the digital age" and suggested that it should be rethought completely[184]. By denying Fourth Amendment protection to expressive and associational data processed by third parties, including communications information and data stored in the cloud, "the third-party doctrine" has created a privacy gap. The gulf continues to widen as information technology advances and third-party records proliferate. No action has been taken by Congress to fill the void. There are laws governing online privacy that are older than the Internet itself.

In this context, the US Supreme Court stepped in and provided case law to fill the void. In its landmark decision of *Carpenter v. United States* has the potential to establish a new interpretation of Fourth Amendment law. In *Carpenter*, the Court considered how the Fourth Amendment applies to location data generated by cell phones when they connect to nearby cell towers. In *Carpenter,* the ACLU's legal argument focused on where Timothy Carpenter had travelled with his phone. Without a warrant, the police obtained Carpenter's detailed location data from his cellphone company (utilising defence of the third party doctrine as the data had passed to the cellphone company allowing the Police to access it). The police were in search of evidence linking Carpenter to various robberies. As a result, Carpenter's daily routines, such as where he slept and where he attended church, were revealed.

The US Supreme Court ruled that the government violated the Fourth Amendment when it demanded seven days of location information from Timothy Carpenter's cell phone provider without a warrant[185]. The decision sits at the intersection of two lines of cases: those that examine location tracking technologies, like beepers or the Global Positioning System (GPS), and those that examine what level of privacy is reasonable for information that is disclosed to third parties, such as banks or phone companies. It was the first time the Fourth Amendment protected location information maintained by a third party, as the Court ruled that a warrant was required.

Furthermore, the court held that the government had access to detailed location data that allows for "near-perfect surveillance." It recognized that the Fourth Amendment protects such sensitive information. It said that Old-world legal rules do not automatically apply to the digital

---

[184] United States v. Jones, 132 S.Ct. 945, 957 (2012) (Sotomayor, J., concurring).

[185] https://www.law.cornell.edu/supremecourt/text/16-402

age. This decision is one of the most consequential decisions regarding privacy for US citizens. In addition to protecting sensitive data from warrantless government intrusions, it also provides guidelines to lower courts.

Upon examining the Court's decision in *Carpenter* and its application to data from various technologies, it becomes clear that the courts strive to maintain the balance of power between the people and the government, as enshrined in the Fourth Amendment. This balance is crucial, as the Fourth Amendment was designed to 'place obstacles in the way of a too permeating police surveillance.' Furthermore, in determining the scope of the Constitution's protections for data generated by digital technologies, the courts should consider the five factors outlined in Carpenter: the intimacy and comprehensiveness of the data, the expense of obtaining it, the retrospective window it offers to law enforcement, and whether it was truly shared voluntarily with a third party. This approach underscores the courts' commitment to protecting privacy rights in the digital age.

Carpenter holds that, in the digital age, that the sensitive information of US citizens does not lose Fourth Amendment protections merely because we store it on a "third party" server, such as Google or Dropbox. This is a game-changer.

Another case in 2024, brought by the ACLU in the Georgia Supreme Court argued that older legal doctrines allowing warrantless searches cannot be "mechanically applied" to complex, evolving digital-age contexts. As technology advances and data becomes more accessible, courts should carefully evaluate what protections will be necessary. In that case, Georgia state argued that police should have the authority to obtain - without a warrant - the vast and detailed data cars collect about their drivers and cars[186]. All kinds of data can be collected, from our car's speed and braking data to call records and text history to music preferences and GPS coordinates[187]. Police do not need a warrant to search a vehicle for physical items under the dated doctrine of "vehicle exemption" due to the "ready mobility" of cars, which might drive away before a warrant is obtained[188]. It was argued by the ACLU that this old rule shouldn't be extended to override people's unprecedented privacy interest in new kinds of sensitive digital data.

---

[186] https://www.wired.com/story/car-data-privacy-toyota-honda-ford/

[187] https://www.eff.org/deeplinks/2024/03/how-figure-out-what-your-car-knows-about-you-and-opt-out-sharing-when-you-can

[188] https://www.law.cornell.edu/wex/automobile_exception

A similar case was brought by the ACLU challenging the US government's warrantless searches of electronic devices at the U.S. border[189]. Until recently, the US federal government has been invoking a centuries-old rule permitting border agents to search travellers' luggage without individualized suspicion or a warrant for contraband or import violations[190]. At ports of entry such as international airports and land checkpoints, US border agents have had virtually unfettered access to Americans and others entering the country[191]. And the problem is only getting worse. The United States Customs and Border Protection (CBP) conducted 33,295 searches of electronic devices in fiscal year 2018[192] —an increase of over six-fold from fiscal year 2012. Furthermore, border searches of electronic devices are not only targeted at bad actors. A wide variety of innocent people have been targeted.

Another recent case concerns the Drug Enforcement Administration's efforts to access—without a warrant—people's prescription records stored in the New Hampshire Prescription Drug Monitoring Program[193]. This secure state-run database is used for public health. The Drug Enforcement Authority argued that when people reveal their symptoms to their doctor and bring the doctor's prescription to their pharmacist, they have given up their Fourth Amendment privacy rights to that sensitive health information[194].

It is a positive development that the Courts in the US are beginning to step in to address these concerns, but progress is slow. In the digital age, avoiding leaving a trail of highly sensitive data is virtually impossible. Our information is saved not only on our laptops and phones but also on the servers of the companies we interact with. It was argued in the First Circuit Court of Appeals that the government can no longer search US citizens' personal information without a warrant. This is by relying on the "third party" doctrine.

Another significant development was the California Consumer Privacy Act (CCPA). Enacted in 2018, the CCPA provides Californian residents with enhanced control over their data. The law grants individuals the right to know what personal information is being collected, the purpose of its use, and the right to opt out of the sale of their data. The CCPA's introduction has set a

---

[189] https://www.aclu.org/press-releases/aclu-and-eff-ask-court-allow-legal-challenge-proceed-against-warrantless-searches

[190] CBP's border searches and confiscations of electronic devices are governed by CBP Directive No. 3340 – 049A, dated January 4, 2018 (the "CBP Policy"). Exh. 19 (CBP 2018 Directive) at § 11, Bates 124

[191] https://www.cbp.gov/border-security/ports-entry

[192] https://www.cbp.gov/newsroom/stats/cbp-enforcement-statistics

[193] https://www.aclu.org/news/privacy-technology/federal-court-says-your-prescription-records-arent-really

[194] https://blog.petrieflom.law.harvard.edu/2018/06/17/prescription-monitoring-programs-hippa-cyber-security-and-privacy/

precedent for comprehensive privacy legislation, inspiring similar efforts in other states and at the federal level.

On the global stage, the European Union's General Data Protection Regulation (GDPR) is a landmark legislative victory for privacy advocates. Enforced in 2018, the GDPR has significantly strengthened privacy protections for EU citizens. The regulation emphasizes transparency, accountability, and individual rights concerning collecting, processing and storing personal data. It introduced stricter consent requirements, the right to access personal data, and enhanced data breach notification obligations. The GDPR has not only had a transformative impact within the EU but has also influenced global privacy standards and inspired similar legislative efforts worldwide.

The Illinois Biometric Information Privacy Act (BIPA)[195] represents a pioneering legislative victory in biometric privacy. Enacted in 2008, the BIPA regulates biometric identifiers' collection, use, and storage, such as fingerprints and facial recognition data. The law requires businesses to obtain informed consent, establish data retention policies, and safeguard biometric information. BIPA's stringent requirements have set a precedent for biometric privacy legislation in other jurisdictions, spurring discussions and legal reforms globally.

In Brazil, privacy advocates achieved a significant victory by passing the Brazilian General Data Protection Law (LGPD)[196]. Enacted in 2018 and modeled after the GDPR, the LGPD establishes comprehensive data protection principles and individual rights. It requires organizations to obtain consent, implement security measures, and provide transparency in data processing. The LGPD empowers individuals with the right to access, rectify, and delete their data, strengthening privacy rights in Brazil and serving as an influential example for privacy legislation in Latin America.

Australia's Privacy Act of 1988[197] is a legislative victory that has helped protect privacy rights in the country. The Act regulates the handling personal information by Australian government agencies and private sector organizations. It sets out privacy principles concerning collecting, using, disclosing, and storing personal data. The Privacy Act of 1988 has been subsequently updated to address new challenges, such as the Notifiable Data Breaches scheme[198], reinforcing privacy protections, and promoting accountability in data handling practices.

---

[195] https://law.justia.com/codes/illinois/chapter-740/act-740-ilcs-14/

[196] https://iapp.org/resources/article/brazilian-data-protection-law-lgpd-english-translation/

[197] https://www.oaic.gov.au/privacy/privacy-legislation/the-privacy-act

[198] https://www.oaic.gov.au/privacy/notifiable-data-breaches/about-the-notifiable-data-breaches-scheme

Despite subsequent technological advancements and the changing communication landscape, the ECPA in the US remains the cornerstone for privacy protections. While it has faced criticism for specific outdated provisions and evolving interpretations, the core principles of the ECPA continue to guide privacy-related legal discussions. The ECPA's provisions requiring warrants for accessing electronic communications have remained relevant and necessary in the face of increasing digital surveillance practices. As new challenges and technologies emerge, lawmakers and privacy advocates continue to assess and advocate for updates to the ECPA to ensure that it effectively protects privacy rights in an ever-evolving digital world.

Legislative victories have played a vital role in fortifying privacy rights, and the Electronic Communications Privacy Act (ECPA) passage is a significant milestone in privacy activism. The ECPA's provisions, particularly those requiring warrants for accessing electronic communications, have established essential safeguards for protecting individuals' privacy. While the ECPA has faced challenges and calls for updates, its enduring significance underscores the ongoing need to balance law enforcement interests with preserving privacy rights. As technology continues to evolve, legislative victories will remain a crucial avenue for advancing privacy protections and ensuring the continued resilience of privacy rights in our modern world.

Privacy activism has evolved as insights and sensitivities developed around safeguarding individual autonomy and dignity. Landmark court cases like Katz v. United States[199] and influential works such as "The Right to Privacy" have laid the groundwork for privacy rights. Developing privacy laws like the GDPR have set new data protection and privacy standards worldwide. Privacy advocates, from Warren and Brandeis to Alan Westin and whistleblowers like Edward Snowden, have played pivotal roles in raising awareness, shaping public discourse, and effecting change. As we navigate the complexities of the modern world, privacy activism remains vital to protecting individual liberties and preserving the delicate balance between technology and personal privacy.

Current political movements for privacy

Privacy advocacy has emerged as crucial voices in safeguarding individual liberties. To explore this we need to shed light on contemporary political movements that champion privacy rights. It highlights prominent organizations such as the Electronic Frontier Foundation (EFF)[200], the

---

[199] https://en.wikipedia.org/wiki/Katz_v._United_States

[200] https://www.eff.org/

American Civil Liberties Union (ACLU)[201], and Privacy International[202]. By exploring their goals, initiatives, and campaigns, we gain insight into the ongoing efforts to protect privacy rights, combat surveillance practices, and advocate for privacy-centric policies. Additionally, we will delve into the intersection of technology and privacy, addressing issues such as digital rights, data protection, and online privacy.

Electronic Frontier Foundation (EFF)

The Electronic Frontier Foundation (EFF) stands as a formidable champion in the realm of privacy advocacy. Since its establishment in 1990, the EFF has remained resolute in its mission to safeguard civil liberties in the digital world. The group has a strong dedication to defending digital rights, challenging government surveillance, and protecting user privacy. Through strategic litigation, policy advocacy, and empowering individuals with resources and tools, the EFF serves as a stalwart defender of privacy rights. The EFF's roots trace back to a time when the internet was still in its infancy, and the need for strong advocates to protect civil liberties became apparent. Founded in 1990 by visionary activists, the EFF emerged as a vanguard organization championing digital rights and privacy in the face of advancing technology and emerging challenges. Throughout its history, the EFF has remained steadfast in its commitment to defending the rights of individuals in the ever-evolving digital realm.

The organization tackles an array of issues at the forefront of privacy advocacy. Through strategic litigation, the EFF challenges privacy infringements in court, setting legal precedents and advancing the cause of privacy. Simultaneously, the organization engages in policy advocacy, working with lawmakers and regulatory bodies to shape privacy-centric legislation and regulations. By advocating for user privacy, the EFF empowers individuals and organizations to protect their personal data from unwarranted surveillance and intrusion.

Recognizing the importance of individual agency in the protection of privacy, the EFF provides a wealth of resources and tools to empower users in the digital realm. This section delves into the EFF's initiatives such as "Surveillance Self-Defense" and "Fix It Already," which aim to educate individuals about privacy threats and provide practical guidance for protecting their digital lives. By equipping users with knowledge and tools, the EFF empowers individuals to navigate the complex landscape of privacy, enhancing their ability to make informed decisions and protect their personal information. The EFF's impact extends beyond the courtroom and the legislative sphere. We need to highlight the organization's commitment to raising awareness and mobilizing action through public campaigns and initiatives. By leveraging the power of

---

[201] https://www.aclu.org/

[202] https://privacyinternational.org/

communication and advocacy, the EFF aims to reach a broader audience, educate the public about privacy concerns, and inspire collective action. Through its campaigns, the EFF sheds light on the implications of intrusive surveillance practices and urges individuals to join the fight for robust privacy protections.

Recognizing the strength in unity, the EFF actively collaborates with like-minded organizations and coalitions to amplify its impact. The importance of collaboration in privacy advocacy needs to be emphasised, highlighting the EFF's partnerships and collective efforts with other advocacy groups. By forging alliances, sharing resources, and working together, these organizations create a unified front against privacy infringements. Collaboration enables the EFF to leverage the collective strength of the privacy community, amplifying its influence and fostering a broader movement for privacy rights.

The American Civil Liberties Union (ACLU)

For over a century, the American Civil Liberties Union (ACLU)[203] has been at the forefront of defending civil liberties, including the fundamental right to privacy. With a legacy of landmark cases challenging government surveillance programs and advocating for privacy rights, the ACLU has established itself as a stalwart defender of individual freedoms. Through litigation, public education, and advocacy efforts, the ACLU plays a vital role in safeguarding privacy, promoting transparency, and holding government surveillance practices accountable.

The ACLU's history is intertwined with the very fabric of civil liberties in the United States. The organization has a century-long legacy, highlighting its unwavering commitment to protecting individual freedoms, including privacy rights. From its inception, the ACLU has tirelessly advocated for the rights of individuals, standing up against unconstitutional intrusions and overreach by the government. Over the years, the ACLU's dedication to safeguarding privacy has become a cornerstone of its mission. The organization has been at the forefront of challenging government surveillance programs that encroach upon privacy rights[204]. We will explore the organization's pivotal role in landmark cases aimed at curbing unconstitutional surveillance practices. From challenging warrantless wiretapping to combating bulk data collection, the ACLU has fought to uphold the Fourth Amendment's protections against unreasonable searches and seizures. Through strategic litigation, the organization has pushed for judicial oversight, transparency, and accountability in government surveillance activities.

---

[203] https://www.aclu.org/news/privacy-technology/supreme-courts-most-consequential-ruling-privacy-digital

[204] https://www.aclunc.org/fighting-high-tech-government-surveillance

The ACLU has consistently stood against law enforcement practices that threaten privacy and civil liberties. The organization has done much to combat overreach, advocating for stronger privacy protections for all individuals, including marginalized communities. Whether challenging invasive surveillance tactics, fighting against unwarranted searches, or advocating for police accountability, the ACLU plays a vital role in safeguarding privacy rights and ensuring that law enforcement practices align with constitutional safeguards. In addition to litigation, the ACLU recognizes the power of public education and advocacy in shaping the narrative and raising awareness about privacy rights. The organization initiatives are primarily aimed at informing and empowering the public. Through public education campaigns, reports, and resources, the ACLU provides individuals with the knowledge and tools necessary to navigate the complex landscape of privacy. By engaging in advocacy efforts, the ACLU amplifies the voices of those affected by privacy infringements, advocates for policy reforms, and works towards a more privacy-conscious society.

Transparency and accountability are key tenets of the ACLU's work in defending privacy rights. The organization aims to hold government agencies accountable for their surveillance practices. The ACLU advocates for transparency in government surveillance activities, fights for the release of relevant information through Freedom of Information Act (FOIA) requests, and challenges excessive secrecy that undermines privacy rights. By shedding light on the practices of government surveillance, the ACLU promotes informed public debate and accountability.

Privacy International

Privacy International is a global organization that works to protect privacy rights and fight against the proliferation of surveillance technologies. Founded in 1990, Privacy International focuses on advocating for stronger privacy laws, raising awareness about surveillance risks, and challenging invasive surveillance practices. The organization conducts research, engages in strategic litigation, and collaborates with partners worldwide to promote privacy-centric policies. Privacy International emphasizes the importance of privacy as a fundamental right and seeks to empower individuals and communities to protect their privacy in an increasingly digital world.

Initiatives and Campaigns

The aforementioned organizations spearhead numerous initiatives and campaigns to protect privacy rights and address the challenges posed by emerging technologies. Some broad campaign themes are;

Campaign Theme 1 - Surveillance Reform: These organizations actively advocate for surveillance reform, calling for greater transparency, accountability, and oversight of government surveillance programs. They push for robust legal frameworks that balance national security concerns with the protection of individual privacy.

Campaign Theme 2- Data Protection and Privacy Laws: Privacy advocacy groups are instrumental in promoting the development and implementation of comprehensive data protection and privacy laws. They work towards ensuring individuals have control over their personal data, promoting transparency in data collection practices, and advocating for stringent safeguards against data breaches.

Campaign Theme 3 - Technology and Privacy: Privacy advocates address the intersection of technology and privacy, raising awareness about digital rights, data privacy, and online surveillance. They push for user-friendly privacy tools, encryption standards, and advocate for policies that prioritize user privacy and protect against unwarranted data collection.

Campaign Theme 4 - Corporate Accountability: These organizations actively campaign for corporate accountability regarding data collection and user privacy. They push for fair and transparent data practices, advocate for user consent and control over personal data, and challenge data-sharing agreements that infringe upon privacy rights.

Contemporary political movements for privacy recognize the significant impact of technology on individual privacy. They tackle issues such as:

Issue 1 - Online Privacy: Advocacy groups promote policies and practices that protect online privacy. They address concerns related to online tracking, data profiling, and intrusive surveillance on digital platforms.

Issue 2 - Digital Rights: Privacy advocates strive to protect and uphold digital rights, including freedom of expression, access to information, and the right to anonymity online. They work to ensure that technological advancements do not infringe upon these fundamental rights.

Issue 3 - Artificial Intelligence and Surveillance Technologies: Political movements for privacy monitor the development and deployment of artificial intelligence (AI) and surveillance technologies. They call for transparency, accountability, and ethical considerations to prevent the erosion of privacy rights in the name of technological advancements.

Contemporary political movements for privacy play a crucial role in defending privacy rights. The previous mentioned organisation are at the forefront of this effort. Through their initiatives, campaigns, and advocacy work, they strive to protect individual privacy, challenge invasive surveillance practices, and advocate for privacy-centric policies. As technology continues to evolve, these movements address the intersection of technology and privacy, championing digital rights, data protection, and online privacy. By actively engaging in the political sphere, these organizations help shape policies and legal frameworks that prioritize privacy and ensure that individuals' rights are protected in an increasingly connected world.

Individuals concerned about privacy can play an active role in political movements dedicated to safeguarding privacy rights. By actively participating, individuals can contribute to effecting change and shaping the discourse surrounding privacy. It is important to move from admiring the problem to action and so we now turn to providing practical advice on how to get involved, outlining various avenues for participation, emphasizing the power of collective action, and highlighting the role of technology in facilitating engagement.

Joining advocacy groups

Joining advocacy groups emerges as a powerful avenue for individuals to make a meaningful impact. We will explore the significance of joining advocacy groups and the transformative potential it holds. By aligning with organizations such as the Electronic Frontier Foundation (EFF), the American Civil Liberties Union (ACLU), and Privacy International, individuals can contribute their time, skills, and resources towards privacy-centric initiatives. Through membership, individuals gain access to valuable resources, educational materials, and opportunities for grassroots activism, thereby bolstering the collective efforts to safeguard privacy rights.

Advocacy groups serve as beacons of change, rallying individuals who share a common goal: the protection of privacy. By joining these groups, individuals tap into the transformative power of collective action. Together, members form a force that amplifies their voices, bolstering the advocacy efforts and raising the profile of privacy issues in the public sphere. The collective impact of dedicated individuals united under a common cause can drive substantial change.

Joining advocacy groups opens doors to a wealth of resources and educational materials. These organizations equip their members with knowledge, insights, and research on privacy-related issues. By tapping into this wealth of information, individuals gain a deeper understanding of the complexities surrounding privacy rights, enabling them to engage in informed discussions and contribute meaningfully to advocacy efforts. Access to educational resources also empowers individuals to educate others, expanding the circle of awareness and fostering a more privacy-conscious society.

Advocacy groups are at the forefront of grassroots activism, mobilizing individuals to take action and effect change. Through their campaigns, petitions, and lobbying efforts, these organizations drive the momentum necessary to push for privacy-centric policies. By participating in these initiatives, members become active agents of change, working alongside like-minded individuals to advocate for robust privacy protections. We will aim to highlight the diverse array of opportunities available for engagement, including public demonstrations, digital activism, and community. One of the core missions of advocacy groups is to raise public awareness about privacy issues. By joining these organizations, individuals become part of a larger movement dedicated to educating the public and challenging the prevailing narrative. Through media campaigns, public events, and educational programs, advocacy groups ensure that privacy remains at the forefront of public discourse. By playing an active role in these efforts, members become catalysts for change, driving the narrative and expanding the circle of awareness.

Joining advocacy groups provides individuals with a network of like-minded individuals and opportunities for collaboration. By connecting with others who share a passion for privacy rights, members can exchange ideas, share experiences, and leverage collective expertise. These networks foster a sense of camaraderie, allowing individuals to learn from one another and amplify their impact. Collaborative efforts, such as joint campaigns or partnerships with other organizations, strengthen the collective voice and create a unified front in the fight for privacy.

Joining advocacy groups is not a mere transaction but a commitment to sustained engagement and long-term impact. One needs to emphasize the importance of active participation and continued involvement in the activities of these organizations. By dedicating time, skills, and resources, members contribute to the ongoing efforts of advocacy groups, ensuring that privacy remains a priority on the political and social agenda. By fostering a culture of sustained engagement, individuals can help shape the future of privacy rights and secure lasting change.

We are reminded of the transformative power that joining advocacy groups holds. By becoming members of organizations dedicated to privacy rights, individuals unlock the potential for collective action, access to valuable resources, and opportunities for grassroots activism.

Through their involvement, members contribute to the broader movement, raising public awareness, driving campaigns, and shaping the narrative surrounding privacy. Let us embrace the power of joining advocacy groups, uniting forces for privacy and creating a future where privacy rights are safeguarded for the benefit of all.

Participating in protests and demonstrations

Throughout history, protests and demonstrations have served as powerful tools for advocating change and shaping the course of societies. In the realm of privacy rights, participating in rallies and demonstrations becomes a potent means for individuals to make their voices heard and demonstrate their unwavering commitment to protecting privacy. It is important to participate in protests and demonstrations, which highlight a capacity to create a visible presence, stimulate public discourse, generate media attention, and apply pressure on decision-makers to address privacy concerns.

Protests and demonstrations provide a platform for individuals to amplify their voices, expressing their concerns and demanding action. By joining these gatherings focused on privacy rights, individuals add their collective strength to the cause. The sheer presence of passionate individuals united under a common goal signals to decision-makers, law enforcement agencies, and the wider public that privacy matters and demands attention. Each voice, each face, contributes to the strength of the movement. Protests and demonstrations serve as catalysts for public discourse on privacy rights. By taking to the streets, individuals spark conversations, challenge existing narratives, and ignite critical discussions surrounding the importance of privacy in society. These events create a space for open dialogue, allowing diverse perspectives to converge, and highlighting the multifaceted implications of privacy infringements. The resulting discourse generates awareness, fosters understanding, and paves the way for policy changes.

The power of protests and demonstrations lies in their ability to capture media attention. By organizing and participating in these events, individuals ensure that privacy concerns gain visibility in the public eye. Media coverage amplifies the reach of the message, disseminating it to a broader audience. News outlets, journalists, and social media platforms become conduits for spreading awareness, extending the impact beyond the immediate physical presence of the protesters. Media attention serves to inform the public, galvanize support, and hold decision-makers accountable. Protests and demonstrations apply pressure on decision-makers, compelling them to address privacy concerns. The sheer scale and intensity of these gatherings create a sense of urgency, urging policymakers to take action. The visibility and public pressure generated by protests can influence the political agenda, forcing policymakers to consider privacy as a priority and driving them towards implementing privacy-centric policies. By making their voices heard, individuals play an instrumental role in shaping the trajectory of policy decisions.

It is important to emphasize that protests and demonstrations for privacy rights are rooted in peaceful and inclusive activism. The strength of these gatherings lies in their ability to bring together individuals from diverse backgrounds and perspectives. Peaceful demonstrations allow for the expression of grievances while maintaining a constructive and inclusive atmosphere. Respect for the principles of non-violence, inclusivity, and diversity ensures that the message remains focused and resonates with a wide range of individuals.

Participating in protests and demonstrations is not a momentary act, but a commitment to sustaining momentum and driving long-term impact. The importance of continuous engagement, fostering connections with like-minded individuals, and collaborating with advocacy organizations is critical. By nurturing relationships and staying involved, participants contribute to the ongoing efforts to protect privacy rights, amplifying their impact and ensuring that the fight for privacy endures beyond a single event.

By joining these gatherings focused on privacy rights, individuals add their voices to a collective force demanding change. The visible presence, public discourse, media attention, and pressure on decision-makers sparked by these events can shape the trajectory of privacy protections. Let us embrace the power of peaceful and inclusive activism, participating in protests and demonstrations to amplify our voices and inspire the change we seek. Together, united in our commitment to privacy, we can pave the way for a future where privacy is valued, protected, and cherished.

Contacting elected officials - amplifying voices for privacy

In the grand tapestry of democracy, the power to shape policy lies in the voices of the people that lawmakers represent. Engaging with elected officials provides individuals with a powerful avenue to make a difference and advocate for privacy-friendly legislation. In a democratic society, the power of the people is the driving force behind policy change. Contacting elected officials allows individuals to actively participate in the legislative process, expressing their concerns, sharing their perspectives, and advocating for robust privacy protections. By engaging in dialogue with policymakers, citizens contribute to the development of laws and regulations that align with their privacy values and address emerging challenges.

Contacting elected officials is not an abstract endeavor; it is a tangible means of connecting with those who have the power to enact change. There are various avenues available for direct communication, such as writing letters, making phone calls, and attending town hall meetings. These channels provide opportunities for individuals to express their thoughts, provide input, and establish personal connections with their representatives.

When contacting elected officials, personal stories become powerful tools for advocacy. By sharing experiences that highlight the importance of privacy in their lives, individuals can humanize the impact of legislation on everyday citizens. Personal narratives can illustrate the real-life consequences of inadequate privacy protections or the transformative potential of strong privacy legislation. These stories resonate with policymakers and can influence their decision-making process. Contacting elected officials is not merely an exercise in venting frustrations; it is an opportunity to influence policy decisions. By articulating the significance of privacy and its essential role in a democratic society, individuals can shape the legislative agenda. They can urge policymakers to support privacy-friendly initiatives, endorse existing bills, or propose new ones. Through respectful and informed communication, citizens can exert their influence and contribute to the adoption of robust privacy protections.

While individual engagement is crucial, collective action amplifies the impact of contacting elected officials. Joining forces with like-minded individuals, advocacy groups, or grassroots movements strengthens the voice of privacy advocates. Forming coalitions, writing joint letters, or organizing community meetings can garner greater attention and create a united front in advocating for privacy-friendly policies. Collaboration maximizes the chances of capturing policymakers' attention and mobilizing broader support. Contacting elected officials should not be a one-time endeavor; it requires ongoing commitment and sustained advocacy. It is important to remain vigilant and monitor ongoing policy developments related to privacy. Staying informed about legislative proposals, attending hearings, and responding to calls for public input ensures that privacy concerns remain at the forefront of the political agenda. Through persistent engagement, individuals can foster long-lasting relationships with elected officials and contribute to a continuous dialogue on privacy issues.

Harnessing the power of grassroots movements - unleashing the force of change

In the grand tapestry of societal transformation, grassroots movements have emerged as powerful agents of change. History has shown us time and time again the remarkable potential of grassroots movements in advocating for privacy rights. By mobilizing communities, fostering dialogue, and building a collective voice, individuals can harness the power of grassroots movements to raise awareness, foster solidarity, and drive meaningful change at local and national levels.

At the heart of grassroots movements lies the strength of community mobilization. By fostering a sense of shared purpose and empowering individuals to take action, grassroots movements can rally communities around the cause of privacy rights. Encouraging discussions within local neighbourhoods, organizing community meetings, and collaborating with like-minded individuals create a ripple effect, igniting a fire of awareness and inspiring collective action.

Grassroots movements thrive on open and inclusive dialogue. By facilitating conversations and encouraging critical thinking, individuals can build bridges of understanding and break down barriers to privacy advocacy. Organizing workshops, town halls, and community forums provides spaces for individuals to learn, share experiences, and explore the nuances of privacy rights. These dialogues foster a sense of empowerment, fuelling the momentum necessary for driving change. The power of grassroots movements lies in their ability to foster solidarity among individuals who share a common cause. When like-minded individuals join forces, their collective voice amplifies, garnering attention and challenging the status quo. Through collaborative efforts, such as forming privacy-focused coalitions or joining grassroots organizations, individuals can harness the strength of unity, creating a force that policymakers cannot ignore.

Grassroots movements have the power to shine a spotlight on privacy rights, raising awareness among communities and challenging the prevailing narrative. By engaging in grassroots activities, individuals become advocates, spreading knowledge and promoting the importance of privacy. From grassroots campaigns and public demonstrations to community-led initiatives, these movements capture public attention, capturing hearts and minds, and inspiring others to take action. While grassroots movements often begin at a local level, their impact can ripple far beyond community boundaries. By focusing on local issues, individuals can highlight the broader implications of privacy infringements and spur change at regional, national, and even international levels. By building alliances with other grassroots movements and collaborating with established advocacy organizations, individuals can create a network that transcends geographic limitations, amplifying their impact and effecting change on a larger scale.

Grassroots movements are not fleeting phenomena but seeds of change that require nurturing for long-term impact. Advocacy efforts need to be sustained, maintaining momentum, and nurturing grassroots movements beyond initial mobilization. By establishing networks, fostering leadership, and developing sustainable strategies, individuals can ensure the longevity and effectiveness of grassroots advocacy for privacy rights.

By mobilizing communities, fostering dialogue, and building solidarity, individuals can unleash the force of change in the realm of privacy rights. Through increased awareness, advocacy, and collective action, grassroots movements have the potential to shape the narrative surrounding privacy at both local and national levels. Let us embrace the power of community mobilization, harnessing the strength of grassroots movements to pave the way for a future that values and protects privacy for all.

Technology plays a crucial role in enabling individuals to engage in privacy movements effectively. Social media platforms offer channels to raise awareness and mobilize support for privacy causes. Sharing information, using relevant hashtags, and participating in online campaigns can reach a wider audience and spark meaningful conversations. Additionally, leveraging encryption tools and privacy-focused technologies can safeguard personal information and protect individuals from intrusive surveillance.

The need for legal and regulatory protections

Although progress has been made as outlined, the need for robust legal and regulatory protections for privacy has reached a critical juncture. It is important to explore the importance of safeguarding individual privacy and the potential consequences that arise from failing to do so. With the rapid proliferation of data collection, surveillance practices, and cyber threats, the role of legal and regulatory frameworks becomes paramount in upholding privacy rights and ensuring accountability.

These digital capabilities have transformed the very fabric of privacy, challenging traditional notions and necessitating a comprehensive reevaluation of privacy protections. We will now explore the intricate relationship between technological advancements, personal data collection, and the erosion of privacy boundaries. It underscores the urgent need for legal and regulatory frameworks that can adapt to the evolving landscape and effectively address emerging privacy challenges. Privacy is an inherent aspect of individual autonomy and human dignity. Privacy is a fundamental pillar of human rights and personal freedom. Robust legal and regulatory protections ensure that individuals have control over their personal information, can make informed decisions about its use, and can maintain autonomy over their own lives. Without such protections, individuals face the risk of exploitation, manipulation, and infringements upon their fundamental rights.

Legal and regulatory protections serve as a critical mechanism for ensuring accountability and transparency in the realm of privacy. Legal and regulatory frameworks help in both public and private entities being held accountable for their data handling practices, surveillance activities, and compliance with privacy standards. It emphasizes the need for robust mechanisms that enable individuals to seek redress, facilitate independent oversight, and promote transparency in the collection, use, and sharing of personal information.

In an interconnected world, privacy knows no boundaries. It is important to underscored the importance of international cooperation in establishing harmonized legal and regulatory frameworks that transcend geographical limitations. It explores the challenges and opportunities of cross-border data transfers, international data sharing agreements, and the harmonization of privacy standards. International cooperation enhances the effectiveness of legal and regulatory protections by fostering collaboration, knowledge-sharing, and the promotion of global privacy norms.

There is an the urgent need for robust legal and regulatory protections in safeguarding privacy rights. In the face of ever-advancing technologies, pervasive data collection practices, and growing surveillance capabilities, legal frameworks play a crucial role in upholding privacy as a fundamental right. These need to establish clear boundaries, fostering transparency and accountability, and promoting international cooperation. By fortifying privacy protections through comprehensive legal and regulatory frameworks, we can navigate the . with confidence, preserving individual autonomy, dignity, and the inherent right to privacy.

The landscape of privacy laws and regulations

As outlined previously, privacy laws and regulations is essential in assessing the state of privacy protections worldwide. This section provides an overview of key legislative developments in the areas already explored. Notably, the EU's General Data Protection Regulation (GDPR) stands as a groundbreaking example, setting a global standard for data protection and individual privacy rights and an ongoing basis for dialogue and development. California's Consumer Privacy Act (CCPA) also continues to garner attention for its stringent privacy provisions and proposals for expansion of coverage to empower residents with increased control over their personal data. Furthermore, the Australian Privacy Act demonstrates efforts to address privacy concerns through comprehensive data protection laws and a basis for review and expansion of privacy rights.

Changes underway in various countries

Countries across the globe are actively responding to the evolving privacy landscape by enacting legislative and regulatory changes, or expanding those rights already in place. This section explores specific initiatives aimed at protecting privacy, ranging from updates to existing laws to the creation of new regulatory frameworks. For instance, the proposed US Privacy Act seeks to establish a federal standard for privacy protections, addressing gaps in the existing patchwork of regulations. The Brazilian General Data Protection Law (LGPD) serves as a significant milestone, aligning Brazil with global privacy standards and emphasizing the rights of individuals over their personal data. In India, the Personal Data Protection Bill is being introduced to address data protection challenges and establish comprehensive privacy regulations.

Challenges and limitations

However, the rapid pace of technological advancements poses challenges to lawmakers, as new data collection practices and privacy concerns continually emerge. Additionally, the cross-border nature of data flows necessitates global cooperation and harmonization of privacy regulations to ensure consistent protections for individuals worldwide. Balancing privacy rights with legitimate interests, such as national security and innovation, presents another challenge, requiring careful deliberation and a nuanced approach.

Concluding Remarks - Privacy, a right for all.

I hope that readers of this book have not succumbed to despair! Rather it should be considered as an outline of the dangers and the positive steps already taken. Having said that, there are still significant challenges in privacy that are a result of the ability of the underlying technology to share data across platforms, agencies, and geographies. These issues are becoming more prevent in our ever growing interconnected world. In this context, the book is a call to embrace ongoing vigilance and collective action. Developments to date hold the promise of progress and the preservation of individual privacy in the face of mounting challenges, however, things could change quickly if continued efforts are not made.

The struggle to protect privacy is an ongoing battle. This reinforces the crucial need for ongoing vigilance among individuals, advocacy groups, and government bodies. The implementation of privacy regulations requires unwavering commitment and active participation from all stakeholders. By remaining vigilant and united, we can ensure the effective enforcement of privacy regulations, creating a safer and more secure environment for all.

No single entity can tackle the complexities of privacy protection alone. This underscores the importance of ongoing collaboration among individuals, organizations, and government bodies. Through shared knowledge, expertise, and resources, we can amplify our efforts and achieve meaningful change. Advocacy groups so far have led the effort by playing a vital role in raising awareness, fostering public discourse, and holding governments and corporations accountable. However, governments must put more effort into these issues, striving to strike a balance between national security and privacy rights, heeding the concerns of their constituents and ensuring transparent governance. While the challenges in safeguarding privacy may appear daunting, there are glimmers of hope. Real progress has been made through legal and regulatory changes. Legislative measures, such as the European Union's General Data Protection Regulation (GDPR) and California's Consumer Privacy Act (CCPA), and emerging case law such in the United States. These have all laid a foundation for enhanced privacy protections. These developments demonstrate that change is possible, and that the collective voice of individuals can influence policy decisions.

Privacy protection is not a static destination but an ongoing journey, and as such our efforts must remain agile and adaptive. We must continuously monitor and assess the efficacy of existing privacy regulations, making necessary adjustments to address emerging challenges. By remaining attentive to technological advancements and proactively updating legal frameworks, we can ensure that privacy protections keep pace with the ever-changing landscape.

In closing, I hope this book has provided a sense of what I see as our collective responsibility to safeguard privacy in the modern age. Hopefully it acts as reminder that the path ahead may be arduous, but it is not insurmountable. Through ongoing vigilance, collaboration, and a commitment to progress, we can forge a future that respects and protects individual privacy. It is a call to action for individuals, organizations, and governments alike to rise to the challenge and create a world where privacy is not a luxury, but a fundamental right for all.

Further reading beyond citations in the text

Adams, C. (2021). *Introduction to privacy enhancing technologies: A Classification-Based Approach to Understanding PETs*. Springer.

Bakir, V., & McStay, A. (2017). Fake News and The Economy of Emotions. *Digital Journalism, 6*(2), 154–175. https://doi.org/10.1080/21670811.2017.1345645

Blum, William (2006). Rogue State: A Guide to the World's Only Superpower. Zed Books Ltd.

Book reviews. (2006). *Totalitarian Movements and Political Religions, 7*(3), 379–396. https://doi.org/10.1080/14690760600819549

Chochia, A., & Nässi, T. (2021). Ethics and emerging technologies – facial recognition. *IDP, 34*, 1–12. https://doi.org/10.7238/idp.v0i34.387466

Danchev, A. (2015). Troublemakers: Laura Poitras and the problem of dissent. *International Affairs*. https://doi.org/10.1111/1468-2346.12241

Edition, S. (2021). *SUMMARY - Citizen four By Laura Poitras*. Shortcut Edition.

Esen, B., & Gumuscu, S. (2016). Rising competitive authoritarianism in Turkey. *Third World Quarterly, 37*(9), 1581–1606. https://doi.org/10.1080/01436597.2015.1135732

French, M., & Smith, G. J. D. (2016). Surveillance and embodiment. *Body & Society, 22*(2), 3–27. https://doi.org/10.1177/1357034x16643169

Greenwald, G. (2014a). *No place to Hide: Edward Snowden, the NSA, and the U.S. Surveillance State.* http://ci.nii.ac.jp/ncid/BB18766657

Greenwald, G. (2014b). *No place to hide: Edward Snowden, the NSA and the Surveillance State.* Penguin UK.

Macnish, K. (2017). *The ethics of surveillance: An Introduction.* Routledge.

Margetts, H. (2018). 9. Rethinking Democracy with Social Media. *The Political Quarterly, 90*, 107–123. https://doi.org/10.1111/1467-923x.12574

Price, D. H. (2014). The New Surveillance Normal: NSA and Corporate Surveillance Age of Global Capitalism. *Monthly Review, 66*(3), 43. https://doi.org/10.14452/mr-066-03-2014-07_3

Rothstein, B., & Teorell, J. (2008). What is quality of government? A theory of impartial government institutions. *Governance, 21*(2), 165–190. https://doi.org/10.1111/j.1468-0491.2008.00391.x

Sesay, A. (2021). *Framing the Cambridge Analytica-Facebook scandal in U.S. and U.K. newspapers: A Quantitative Content Analysis.*

Snowden, E. (2019). *Permanent record*. Metropolitan Books.

Soldatov, A., & Borogan, I. (2013). Russia's surveillance state. *World Policy Journal*, *30*(3), 23–30. https://doi.org/10.1177/0740277513506378

Steen, M., & Thomas, M. (2015). *Mental health across the lifespan: A Handbook.*

Routledge. Voigt, P., & Von Dem Bussche, A. (2017). The EU General Data Protection Regulation (GDPR). In *Springer eBooks*. https://doi.org/10.1007/978-3-319-57959-7

Weckert, J. (2005). *Electronic monitoring in the workplace: Controversies and Solutions.* IGI Global.

Wright, D., & Kreissl, R. (2014). *Surveillance in Europe*. Routledge.

Zarsky, T. (2019). Privacy and manipulation. *Theoretical Inquiries in Law*, *20*(1), 157–188. https://doi.org/10.1515/til-2019-0006

Zuboff, S. (2019). *The Age of Surveillance Capitalism: The fight for a human future at the new frontier of power*. https://cds.cern.ch/record/2655106

Visit the authors page at

https://www.lulu.com/spotlight/owus/

https://www.amazon.in/stores/Mathew-Henderson/author/B0D281Q3KD?
ref=ap_rdr&isDramIntegrated=true&shoppingPortalEnabled=true

www.ingramcontent.com/pod-product-compliance
Lightning Source LLC
LaVergne TN
LVHW072049060326
832903LV00053B/302